PAST LIFE RECOVERY

INGRID VALLIERES

Past Life
Recovery

Translated by
PAT CAMPBELL

ASHGROVE PRESS, BATH

First published in Great Britain by
ASHGROVE PRESS LIMITED
Bath Road, Norton St Philip
Bath BA3 6 LW

Originally published in German
under the title
Praxis der Reinkarnationstherapie

Originally published in English as
Reincarnation Therapy

ISBN 1–85398–104–4

This edition published 1998

Typeset in 10/11½ Palatino by
Ann Buchan (Typesetters), Middlesex
Printed and bound in Great Britain by
Redwood Books, Trowbridge, Wiltshire

CONTENTS

PAST LIFE RECOVERY

Foreword

The idea that our former lives may be the cause of problems in our present life is not new, but only in the last few years have we seen the development of a practical therapeutic method. Reincarnation has long been accepted as fact in the life and thought of many people, but its application in tracking down the causes of problems has increasingly come to the fore since therapists have started seeking effective theories and techniques for obtaining models and values based on experience in the solution of problems.

It is not in any way our aim to prove the existence of former lives, but rather just to allow this immense potential of unconscious material the right to exist. No satisfactory answers have as yet been found to many human questions. This kind of approach gives a perspective on timeless nature and the constantly repeating history, which a man creates during a lifetime.

Preoccupation with former lives can take the philosophic form of meditatively considering a person's endless possibilities and his creative potential. However, reincarnation therapy goes even further than this in investigating the features of one's own character, one's own tendencies and ways of thought, in order to deepen in this way one's understanding of human emotions and reactions.

My experience in this field has shown me that there are in the world various therapists, who have laid foundation stones for the propagation of this therapy. These therapists have shown sincerity and competence in introducing this therapy to specialists and non-specialists alike. Both in public lectures and in private sessions, they have demonstrated the constant effectiveness of this method. Many people have in their later therapy sessions been able to alter their lives fundamentally in a positive direction. In spite of some occasional attacks and criticisms, these therapists have succeeded in carrying out their intentions, thereby justifying their faith.

One of these people is Ingrid Vallieres. Our mutual work has revealed her great insight and talent, together with her sincere sympathy and understanding of all who meet her. Her knowledge and experience are a treasure for the field of reincarnation therapy and for those who wish to follow her example.

In these pages the reader will find a clear and concrete presentation of facts and examples, demonstrating the ability with which she has been working all these years.

Sceptics will find their doubts challenged, those with an open mind will be encouraged. Everyone can profit from the experience and knowledge of Ingrid Vallieres.

Norris Netherton Ph.D.

Introduction

The desire to enlighten the darkness of understanding is as old as humankind. Understanding? That is what happens to me when I die. As long as our world of the senses remained unexplored, as long as there was no natural science or technology, the world beyond our senses was visible to the eyes of man and the sky was bright and clear. It followed that no one doubted there being a life after death. However, since the face of our awareness has fundamentally changed, since it has been possible to explore and explain the earth right down to the very last atom, the 'spiritual' horizon has dimmed. In other words, as this lifetime was illuminated, the hereafter became obscure. As a result various explanations of the nature and meaning of death and the hereafter have emerged.

The scientist's answer is the simplest: Death is the ultimate end of a living organism, the arrival at the outermost bounds, where all life functions cease. There is no life hereafter just as there can be none before the present lifetime. One senses the inadequacy of this statement, which implies that there is no difference between plant, animal and human death. According to their nature, however, they are all extremely different. When the leaves of trees fall to the ground in the autumn and plants wither and die from the frost, one might speak of nature dying. Yet in reality death is here as Goethe describes: 'Nature's cunning way of having many lives', for not a single leaf falls from the branch of a tree without first forming a bud and with it the guarantee of new life in the spring.

The death of man, however, is a unique occurence. When every endeavour to cure an illness, every possible attempt today at resuscitation has failed, and 'clinical death' occurs, then the life of man has reached its ultimate conclusion. The body will shortly decompose and either decay in the ground or be burnt by fire. According to this principle the existence of every molecule or atom can be traced further in the words spoken at the graveside: 'Ashes to ashes, dust to dust'.

That is the external side of dying and of the death of a human being – but the real question concerns the fate of the soul. This, too, has reached a boundary and crossed over it. Its earthly life is plainly over. What comes next? Every boundary has two sides to it – this side and the other side. This is true both of the physical and of the spiritual sphere. We speak of boundaries in all the stages of existence which we know. If a man does not know his own limits, whether it be the boundary with his neighbour's garden or the limit of his own strength, he will suffer the consequences.

The crossing of boundaries is subject to special laws. Anyone who does not pay sufficient attention to them, does so at his peril. Nowadays, as a rule, a person is satisfied if he understands his life within the boundaries of birth and death. The obvious questions: 'what was there before?' 'what will come after?' do certainly arise, but as a rule they are put aside as being unanswerable, or else they are just answered superficially. Either it is pointed out that, after all, no one could possibly know what was before birth and what will be after death, or else people talk about natural events, before birth our parents were there and after death our body will decay. Besides, there is a suspicion that all other assertions are in any case just wishful thinking, helping people to find comfort when faced with the remorselessness of death.

Therefore, in this book I do not want to follow the blind path of proving that there is a life outside our life, but rather I would like to make a constructive attempt to go deeper into the questions, by setting out from the point at which people usually stop asking.

In Buddhism, as in all Indian religions, we find an important symbolism of opposites: ignorance or not-knowing and knowledge or the perception of wisdom. Ignorance is not-knowing the true causes underlying the restrictions and limitations under which the 'non-knower' instinctively lives and suffers. Knowledge, in this connection, is clarification of all the tragic manifestations which the soul encounters. Where there is enlightenment and conscious clarification, obstacles, standing in the way of inward liberation, simply disappear.

The more ignorance, or knowledge which is not yet available from the totality of consciousness, can be changed into perception and knowledge, the more concrete knowledge, consciousness and awareness of the present will become. From this point of view so-called reincarnation experiences are meaningless as long as they are to be used as a proof of whether or not there has been existence before life. Such experiences will be significant for the individual only if they produce in him a kind of extension of his consciousness, so that he can recognise what has infiltrated his soul, what has prevented him from being the man he always wanted to be and should have been.

Tracking down these inner infiltrations is the purpose of this book, the deep purpose of my work. My aim is, consequently, clear. It is a question of helping people via an unusual channel to find liberation, through self-knowledge and also beyond the boundaries of their present life. We make this crossing of boundaries entirely consciously, knowing from experience that boundaries, by their very nature, can be extremely restricting.

From his organic and physical structure, man is in the first place a terrestial being and, therefore, tied to natural, instinctive behaviour. His whole corporeality is bound up with biological and natural processes. But man is, at the same time, a spiritual creature, conscious of himself, and as such he recognises another level of his being, in which he can place himself outside and beyond all natural events. The fact that man is bound up in the rhythm of nature is not the problem. This occurs only when the spiritual nature of man becomes self-sufficient and places itself in opposition to his earthly nature. This is the point of departure for a doctrine of suffering, which represents itself as suffering from the world, and manifests itself in the form of physical and mental pain. The spirit often finds it very hard to accept earthly, physiological events, such as illness, material losses, natural catastrophes or the loss of a dear one. Through the suffering it becomes aware that it is not in harmony with the external event, that it lacks deeper understanding and insight into the necessity of these fateful occurrences. Here the person has a presentiment that life will in some hidden way require him to face up to his own limitations and shortcomings and to overcome them.

If we pursue these lines of thought with regard to possible reincarnations, then it necessarily follows that we shall also have to consider the idea of Karma. Karma is personal experience of the fruits of one's own thinking, intentions and actions. It is suffering the consequences of past action and of the attitudes which led up to them; man is, so to speak, the sum total and the result of all his former deeds and decisions.

It is certainly difficult for a Westerner to grasp the idea of Karma, even when he tries to imagine the incredibly harsh consequences. Buddhism teaches that the consequences of one's own actions come under a law which must be obeyed and accords this absolute status, operating as it does outside the limits of a single, individual life. It is the world's own law of causality. It is only in the light of this timelessness that one can grasp the Buddhist theory that man must also bear responsibility for those fateful events which are incomprehensible to him and which he does not believe he could ever have caused. According to Buddhist ideas, the events and troubles of this life derive not only from current or earlier actions in this life, but also from the causes of such actions, which lie in a so-called earlier life. Naturally this theory assumes that the future too, including that of a later earthly existence, can be influenced in a positive or negative way by corresponding behaviour.

Here it is not a question of moral judgments as such, but of behaviour with regard to the wellbeing and development of man and it is only in this sense that there is good and bad Karma. With regard to the state of human consciousness, Buddhism speaks of beneficial and Karmically unbeneficial behaviour. The former leads to the gaining of consciousness and to liberation, the latter to bondage and ignorance.

If there is such a thing as a former life and if Karma plays an important part in it, then in this book I would like, with the aid of many examples, to track down this Karma and the fateful events connected with it. For this purpose it will be necessary to make journeys into the past.

Reincarnation – this subject calls forth the most varied associations: Indian religion, reincarnation as animals, punishment for earlier deeds, a spiritual explanation for poverty and the blows of fortune, opportunities for further development, hope of liberation. . .

However it is by no means necessary to look first to religion and esoterics in order to meet with reincarnation. Each one of us in our everyday life has already had experiences, used sayings and followed trains of thought which point to reincarnation; for example, the attraction and fascination one feels for another person, which borders almost on the magical, or else the deep antipathy to someone, which cannot reasonably be explained in one's present life; or a patient describes his pain to the doctor in words like these: 'It is as though a piece of wire were piercing me through the stomach', 'It is as though I were burning inside', 'My back feels as though it were broken', 'A thousand needles are going through my head.' Many people express fears, such as: 'I am afraid that if I swim out too far from the bank, I shall not come back again,' 'I don't make any long journeys because something bad might happen on one of them', 'I don't dare to contradict anyone, because I usually get the worst of it', 'I feel as though I were being cross-examined.'

Vividly descriptive language derives largely from reincarnative components of our unconscious. Since our unconscious is older than our present identity, there are many inexplicable fears, problems and concepts, which have not originated in our present life. Our present character, our thinking and striving, may be the collective experience of our former lives and we are continually engaged in change, because our store of experience is continually being extended.

My personal encounter with reincarnation was at the age of about eight years. As I listened to the words of the preacher in church, an idea suddenly came into my head: 'I have already been in the world a thousand times.' This realisation seemed to me quite natural. The number a thousand is here not exact, it is just a symbol for the concept reincarnation. When I was twelve years old I bought my first book on yoga and carried out the exercises described in it on my own, which led to many difficulties.

This was followed later by professional courses in yoga and an intense preoccupation with world religions, in which I was drawn chiefly towards Hinduism and Buddhism. At seventeen I made my way to India, coming home with many impressions but also with many disappointed illusions. In my over-eagerness I had placed many too many expectations on the Yogis, some of which were realised and some disappointed. My next journey – by now I was nineteen – took me to Japan, where I devoted myself particularly to Zen-Buddhism. In Japan I immediately felt at home and I learnt the language within a few months. As I was to discover later in my own regressions, I had formerly had some very intense experiences in Japan. This was also the origin of my very active interest in Asian martial arts, which I had begun to practise when I was sixteen. My behaviour at that time towards my martial art friends, who were mostly male, was rather peculiar – in my opinion they were too soft, amateurish and immature, whereas I took the sport in earnest. This attitude was explained in a later regression, in which I lived through the experience of being the male leader of a Japanese martial troop. This was a group of extremely well-disciplined and hardened men, who had placed their lives at the service of the emperor and went round the country in order to seek out spies and enemies of the emperor and to destroy them. There was no place here for sentiment or frivolity, which would have meant death.

When, at the age of twenty, I was lying in hospital, my life in danger with serious burns resulting from an accident, I couldn't help thinking: 'You have experienced this before.' I must already have had the experience of being burnt alive, it was very familiar to me. The accompanying pain and fading of consciousness, until I left my body, reminded me of being burnt at the stake and of being shut up inside a burning, melting machine room. At the height of this crisis I was hovering between life and death. I had already distanced myself a long way from my body and now had scarcely any connection with it. This was a very pleasant situation, being free of everything physical and conscious of eternity; but the realisation came to me like a blow that up to now I had not in any way fulfilled my life's task and that on this account it was absolutely necessary for me to return to my body. After all, what had I achieved? My spiritual development had only just begun and the balance sheet did not exactly look rosy – I had not solved any of my fundamental problems, but had only just begun to concern myself with the purpose of life. It was, therefore, absolutely necessary that I should go back into life, in order to follow the path I had entered upon right to the end. After this abrupt about-turn, this absolute affirmation of life, my body recovered visibly. During the period of convalescence, my life appeared to me as a second chance, it was indeed a new life. I wanted to make good use of this second chance and not to let a moment slip by without getting to know my life's task and working at it until I achieved it.

A year after this accident, I heard for the first time about reincarnation therapy. I was fascinated by the possibility of actually remembering past lives and I decided without more ado to go to the U.S.A. and begin this therapy. The life I had led up to then had certainly not been entirely unsuccessful and yet, in spite of meditation and spiritual exercises, I was suffering from a lack of self-confidence, from melancholy and varying moods. Inner stability was lacking and something was preventing me from living and developing my personality to the full.

After just a few sessions of reincarnation therapy, a new kind of activity and enjoyment of life developed. My problems became comprehensible to me through involvement in former lives and I was able to resolve them without difficulty. Completely new life prospects opened up to me and it became clearer and clearer to me that it is only man himself who is responsible for all his difficulties. And only because he himself is responsible for his fate, can he himself resolve it and alter it.

Towards the end of the therapy, which lasted for two years, I had found myself and could at last live according to my inclination.

The changes in my personality were so fundamentally positive that I decided that I would also take a training in reincarnation therapy, in order to study all the connections of fate and the exact way in which the subconscious works. The theoretical work was supplemented by many hours of practice. In working with others, I gained a deeper understanding of the connection between present fate and past experiences and I was able to observe the law of Karma working out in many people and to experience it with them. Even more important was that others too, through being regressed, were able to recognise their own Karma, to accept it and to alter it. In the final analysis, the task of reincarnation therapy is to recognise what is old and past, to accept it and put an end to it, so that one is not always unconsciously reproducing the past in the present or having to fear it and thus one makes room for a conscious and spontaneous experience of the present and a free and self-determined shaping of the future.

Since then, during the last ten years I have held some 20,000 reincarnation therapy sessions with other people. This work has confirmed me in my belief that we are all free beings, who have got ourselves into difficulties through our own faults and that nothing can happen to us today except what we ourselves have at some time caused. Recognising and accepting this enormous responsibility and discovering in what way we have treated it lightly represents one of the main tasks in reincarnation therapy. Only when we assume responsibility for our present and our past, can we really be free.

Ingrid Vallieres   Stuttgart

1.

Why Reincarnation Therapy Brings Help to Mankind

Thet Somwong, gravedigger in the small market town of Chang-Klang in south Thailand, was most surprised when he was asked by the village schoolmaster Samram Wangpreech what he had done twenty-five years before with the body of his three-month-old daughter. At that time the schoolmaster had begged the gravedigger to bury the child in the Protestant cemetery.

The embarrassed Thet Somwong now had to admit that he had secretly buried the schoolmaster's daughter in the grounds of the nearby temple, in order to spare himself the long journey to the Christian cemetery.

When small children died in the country, people did not usually make a great fuss about it. They would ask the undertaker to arrange an unobtrusive burial and would not worry about the funeral. In the seventies, the fact that after twenty-five years the carelessness of a lazy gravedigger came to light, aroused public interest.

The child who had died at that time had meanwhile been reborn into another family. At the age of twelve she entered a Buddhist convent near to the temple of Wat Thao in the province of Nakhorn Si Thammarat. Pathowan Inthanu had left her large family in order to find inner peace in the convent.

Ten years later in the summer of 1978, Pathomwan was sitting meditating in the shade of a kapok tree. In a state of trance she had an experience which affected her deeply. There appeared to her a room in which she herself was lying on a straw mat. Her body appeared to be quite tiny. She was having difficulty in breathing. Her two parents standing round her were quarrelling all the time. The notes of a xylophone were sounding in her ears. Suddenly the girl felt relief. The heaviness of her body grew less. She felt lighter and lighter and finally reached the state of weightlessness.

What the young nun next experienced in her vision made her shudder. She was floating freely in space and experiencing everything as an onlooker. Her parents were standing in front of the lifeless body of a three-months-old child. A man appeared, wrapped up the corpse in a cloth and carried it away. He stopped at the village temple. Then Pathomwan in her trance saw the man putting the bundle into the hollow of a broken pillar, filling up the hole with stones and going away. Pathomwan felt herself being carried through the air. Suddenly she was floating over a village. An elderly woman was sitting in front of a house cleaning fish. Pathomwan felt herself drawn towards the woman. She approached her and recognised her own mother. Suddenly the nun awoke from her trance, bathed in sweat. No one had observed her. For a year she carried this vision around with her. She did not dare to speak to anyone about it.

Then what she had seen in trance became reality. The man, whom the nun had seen during her meditation, appeared at the convent. He spoke to her and asked why such a pretty girl should spend her life in a convent. She would do better to get to know a man and marry him. Driven by some inner force, Pathomwan allowed herself to be invited to go with the man, who introduced himself as the teacher Samram Wang Preech, to his village which was over a hundred kilometres away.

During the journey the teacher begged the nun to leave the order and become his adopted daughter. Absentmindedly the confused girl stammered that she really was his daughter. The astonished schoolmaster naturally wanted an explanation of this mysterious assertion and now the girl described everything she had seen in her dream. Samram listened to the description open-mouthed. When he reached his native village with the nun, he was terrified to find that the girl knew more than she should have been able to know. She quickly established that it was not the same house in which she had been born 25 years before. She then gave as good a description of the old house as anyone who knew the village well could have given. And when the schoolmaster's wife appeared at the door, the girl, deeply moved, called out 'mother'. The greatest surprise came when the nun led the teacher and his wife to the temple and indicated the exact spot where the gravedigger had hidden the body of the little girl. She continually talked about the circumstances surrounding her previous death and the undignified burial to her astonished new parents. Her story was so exact that finally investigations were made which entirely confirmed the child's words. The young girl was subsequently questioned again by Buddhist monks in Bangkok. Her evidence was recorded on tape, and with that a new and spectacular case of reincarnation became known throughout Thailand. Today it is used by western science as a basis of research.

I would like to use this example to indicate the possibility of reincarnation, particularly since it is a case to which the experts have already paid attention. I have no intention of setting out to *prove* reincarnation, but rather to show by means of various examples that by way of reincarnation therapy, by 'journeys into a distant past', the possibility exists of healing body, mind and spirit.

Reincarnation therapy is based on the fact that suffering, whether it be of the body or of the mind, may be the consequence of a previous life. In the course of such a therapy, old experiences, 'old debts' are discharged, so that the person in question learns to concentrate fully on the present, in order to live in the 'here and now', without being inhibited by a past which has not been worked out. We know from psychosomatic medicine that the spirit has a deep influence on the body. Attacks of asthma, stomach ulcers and intestinal abscesses may be taken as examples of this.

The way that experiences from a former life may affect the present is shown in the example of the forty-five year old widow of a chemist. The tragic part about her present life is that she keeps meeting authoritarian people by whom she is easily intimidated. From this has developed a fear of people. She does not dare to express her own wishes and has difficulty in making decisions. She lives constantly under the fear of being tied down, of being confined in some way if she binds herself by making a decision.

The main event which embraces all these problems was one she experienced on her first regression into a previous life. 'I am a mistress and I am living at Versailles during the rococco period. There I exercise my power gently but relentlessly. I keep whispering things into the King's ear and he does exactly what I want. I am charming, but malicious. If someone is not devoted to me and does not pay me enough attention and appreciate me sufficiently, then this person will lose his position at court. Many courtiers try to set the King against me. They say I am too expensive, I cost the court too much money for jewellery and clothes. They find fault with me for changing my clothes three times a day. But these intrigues against me cost them dearly. I have seen to it that one of the countesses was banished. She had wanted to dispute my rank, to be the King's mistress just like me. I put it to the King that this countess had done something and I was hypocritically asking his advice. I told him that she had stolen some jewellery. I made him think that he had suggested that she should be banished. I always agreed with the King and said what he expected me to say. The King and I always made political decisions together. If anyone agitated against me, I pointed out this person's faults, fastened some crime on him and saw to it that he disappeared from court. I was interested only in luxury and power, I had no sympathy with people without rank. As I became older I had to seek out very young mistresses and introduce them to the King. I always looked for weak, docile girls who did not compete with me. As long as these young women did not hold any emotional sway over the King, I did not mind at all. At some point the King died and I got the power. I had the power because my son, whom I had given to the King, reigned after him. This son was more gently disposed towards the people, but I saw to it that we maintained our power undiminished.

'One day people forced their way into the palace. There were a great many of them. I felt afraid. But a deputation of courtiers calmed them down again. The people complained of too high taxes, of too little food. They demanded that the King should give up his castles. My son and I promised that elections would be introduced. We took some of the citizens into the palace. We let them share in our "good life", we bribed them with gifts. The people allowed themselves to be calmed down, they told the populace that the luxury was not so very great, but the people at large would not be pacified. They gathered full of hatred outside the palace. Someone or other threw out gold coins in order to distract the crowds below. But they would not be restrained and thronged angrily into the palace. There were hundreds of them. They came in and surrounded me, crying "Down with her!" They locked me up in a prison. I felt in a panic. I had never thought that they would go to such lengths. In prison there was no more luxury, I was dirty, my head itched, I got fleas and lice. I had to drink foul water. These damned people spoilt everything for me. It was just their bad luck that they were born into the lower classes. I was born to something higher. I felt self-pity and a sort of narrow-mindedness. At some point I died, completely without insight.'

This example of reincarnation shows significant parallels with the present life of that woman. Afterwards she said to me: 'In my present life, too, I have got quite a few people into hot water, especially my colleagues. I have shown up their faults. Just like the courtiers, my father always accused me of being too expensive. The mistress whom I banished at that time is my mother in my present life. I cannot get rid of her, she is ill and bedridden, I have to look after her. I have to care for her. My daughter is always tormenting me, she is just like I was in those days. She is always trying to impose her will on me. I am rather lazy and would like to have a pleasant life. Perhaps that is why I lost my husband early. If he had not died, I would probably have taken things too easily at his side. Just as the people who broke into the palace terrified me, so I am afraid of people in my present life.'

The Tibetan Book of the Dead (Bardo Thödol) was compiled at the turn of the century from the teachings of wise men, definitively written down in the eighth century A.D. It recounts almost everything we hear today, from those who have been reanimated, about the stages of death, right down to actual details.

The separation of the ego from this material body, the exit of the ego, is the first experience common to these accounts of dying. Lama Gorinda writes in the introduction to the Tibetan Book of the Dead (Evans-Wentz edition): 'Most people are of the opinion that no one who has not himself already died, can speak authentically about death, and since no one has come back from the dead, it is impossible to make any statement about death itself or the situation after death.'

The wise men of Tibet reply: 'There is not a single person, who has not come back from the dead.'

Indeed, we have all died many deaths before we enter upon this life; for what we call birth is nothing but the other side of death, another name for the same process seen from the opposite point of view, just as we describe the same door as the way in and the way out, depending on whether we are looking at it from the outside or the inside of a house or a room.

One might rightly wonder that everyone does not remember his last death; and this is the reason why most people do not believe that they have experienced it. But in the same way they do not remember their birth – and yet they do not for a moment doubt that they were born! They overlook the fact that our active retrieval capacity – that is the memory recall subject to our conscious will – forms only a small part of our normal consciousness and that our 'subconscious memory' registers and stores up all the impressions and experiences which have long since slipped away from our waking consciousness.

There are people who, by reason of their concentration and other yoga practices, are able to raise the contents of the subconscious to the level of the active, discerning, waking consciousness, so that it is possible for them to make use of the wealth of that deep memory, which stores up not only our past existences, but also the past of humanity and of all prehuman forms of life – if not actually that consciousness which first gave rise to the whole life of this universe.

If, through whatever chance of nature, the doors of an individual's deep consciousness were opened too suddenly, the conscious mind would be crushed and destroyed. For this reason, all initiates and knowers advisedly kept the doors of deep consciousness hidden beneath a veil of mystery and symbolism.

Those, however, who possess the power and inner maturity to lift this veil and open the doors, are in a position to penetrate the identity of birth and death and to recognise the continuity and inter-relationship of all life. For them, being born again is not just a theory but an experienced fact, which can be confirmed by every earnest seeker and striver. As for the others – who are not yet in a position to see the unveiled truth – they will, by means of symbols and initiation rituals and the spiritual exercises connected with them, be brought step by step to knowledge and personal experience.

'If there is a natural body, then there is also a spiritual body' writes St Paul in his first Epistle to the Corinthians – which means that we human beings possess that soul body which, in accordance with the teachings of all the great religions, survives the death of the earthly body.

The ancient Egyptians called this second body 'ka', the cabalists called it 'Nepeseh' and the spiritists 'perispirit'. Paracelsus spoke of his starbody or 'astral body', Descartes used the expression 'subtle material' for it, Newton called it 'spiritus subtilissimus'. C.G. Jung wrote that as a doctor he had been able to confirm 'in certain cases, the occurrence of subjectively experienced levitations in moments of specially distressing confusion'. He describes a death experience which he underwent in 1944 after breaking his foot and suffering a heart infection. Whilst he was 'hovering in immediate danger of death and being given oxygen and camphor' Jung had the experience of being in an archetypal body about 1500 kilometres up in space and seeing what only the astronauts were later to see: 'Far below me I saw the terrestrial globe bathed in a glorious blue light. I saw the deep blue sea and the continents. Far below my feet lay Ceylon and before me lay the subcontinent of India. My field of vision did not include the whole earth, but its global shape was clearly recognisable and its contours shimmered in silver through the wonderful blue light.'

Since in former times people appear to have believed unreservedly in a life after death, they always spent a great deal of time preparing for an afterlife. For believers in the great religions of the world, this preparation consisted and still consists in spiritual and moral training to achieve the good.

Among simpler people in prehistoric times the good consisted in having the necessities of life. Thus about fifty thousand years ago the Neanderthal people never buried their dead without food and tools – thus assuming that life after death would not be very different from life on earth. In some of the graves of the Etruscans, whose state flourished long before Rome, even furniture and horse-drawn carts have been found, buried in the hope that they would be useful to the prospective spiritual beings in their new realm.

In ancient civilisations it was laid down that on the death of important persons, extensive preparations should be made for life in the new world, ensuring that the life style on earth would without fail be maintained.

In the twenties of this century archaeologists dug up the royal graves of the city of Ur, which lies in present-day Iraq and people were astounded when they found the grave of Queen Shubad, surrounded by sixty-eight women of her court and armed soldiers. The bodies lay arranged in rows.

It must, however, be assumed that the Queen's servants had taken poison or narcotics before following their Queen into death and being buried with her.

About five hundred years ago, the Incas in South America practised similar rites when their King, whom they considered as a god, was to be buried. Against their will, victims were sent to their deaths with him. After his death, the ruler was embalmed and wrapped in precious cloths. These comparatively well-preserved bodies were then venerated for the very last time as holy relics in a drunken farewell feast. The Incas firmly believed that his soul would enter another world and for this reason his favourite wives and slaves were sent to death with him.

In the grave of an Egyptian nobleman of Thebes, the archaeologists found painted statuettes in the likeness of men, which were supposed to symbolise his slaves. It was thought at that time that the nobleman would awaken them to life again in the new world, so that they could continue to serve him.

The ancient Egyptians concerned themselves much more than other cultures with life after death.

If they had not given their pharaohs and nobles so many objects in their graves, we should not have been able to learn nearly so much about their culture, their lives and their crafts.

The burial chambers of the pyramids, where the pharaohs were buried, held costly paintings, household equipment and jewellery intended to guarantee the pharaoh a pleasant life in the afterworld. A basic principle of the Egyptian faith was that not only would the body of the dead survive, but also the spirit (ka). That is the main reason why the body was so carefully embalmed, that it had the necessary food at its disposal and that food was even brought to it regularly. As time went on, belief in life after death took on a rather more democratically humane note, that is to say this privilege was no longer reserved just for the pharaohs and nobles, but was accorded to the whole population. It was believed that every soul would be judged and in order to obtain this it had to endure an exacting pilgrimage to the abode of the god Osiris, ruler of the underworld.

There in the presence of Osiris and his 42 judges, the heart of the dead person was weighed on the scales of justice. The soul was given the capacity to decide whether the person had been guilty of many sins, such as cruelty to animals or theft of food provided for the dead.

The religion of Zoroaster in ancient Persia had a similar teaching that after death one had to go on a long journey to a place where one would be judged. On the fourth day after death, the human soul had to cross the bridge to the other side. In the middle of this bridge was a sword. Righteous people could cross this bridge without any problem, for them a beautiful maiden was waiting on the other side, symbolising the good deeds performed on earth by the dead person. The righteous were admitted to paradise, where they received rich gifts.

However, if an unrighteous person tried to cross the bridge, it would open up in the middle and the sinner would fall into the depths.

According to the Aztec faith, a person's life on earth also determined the kind of life that he would have in the hereafter. Those who were offered up as a sacrifice to the gods entered automatically into the paradise of the Sun God, where they continued to exist as butterflies or bumblebees. Women who died in childbirth also had this privilege. The fate of everyone else was in a second-class heaven.

In the Koran, the holy book of Islam, there is the description of a rather luxurious paradise. Those whom Allah chose were to recline on jewel-encrusted couches, face to face, and they were to have eternal youth and they were to drink noble wine out of noble vessels. They were to enjoy all the fruit they desired and they were to eat the flesh of fowls and other things besides. And the dark-haired houris would be there – unspotted virgins – as pure as hidden pearls: there no useless chatter would trouble them, no sinful talk, but only words of greeting; 'Peace, peace.'

In contrast to this the wicked will be condemned by Allah to purgatory and there they will receive only boiling water and mould and filth to eat.

The ancient Greeks had various views on life after death. One of the most widespread views was that the soul of the dead person would go down to Hades, where the god Pluto ruled. That was a dark place, where souls vegetated as shades, similar to the fate of Sheol, or the place of lost souls of the Jewish faith.

At the same time the Greeks had at their disposal another Hell, which they called Tartarus and a Heaven known as the Elysian fields. In Heaven the few chosen ones enjoyed eternal spring. This was particularly emphasised by the Orphic sects. These owed their name to Orpheus, who, according to legend, went down to Hell and forced the appropriate god to allow his dead wife Eurydice to go back into life. On his journey back into the upper world, Orpheus was continually checking that the wife whom he had won back to life was following him. However, this was contrary to the strict command of Hades and as a punishment Orpheus lost both his own life and that of his wife.

A further Greek belief was founded on Pythagoras and his mathematical and philosophical teachings. Pythagoras believed that the soul was condemned to live in a body and that it would be reincarnated in another human or an animal body. Pythagoras reported that he himself had existed several times before, among other things as a soldier in the Trojan war.

The strongest belief in the rebirth of the soul was found in Asia. In Hinduism, the religion of the majority of the population of India, the human soul is a reflection of the world soul and it is the aim of every human life to become one with the divine principle. However, before the soul reaches this stage, it must go through many stages of rebirth, both as a human being and also as an animal. The whole circle of rebirths is called the 'wheel of Samsara', and it turns without beginning or end like the universe. The Hindu believes that he can determine the manner of his next rebirth through his Karma, the sum of all the actions in his life on earth. A bad Karma causes him to be born again as a person of low caste, so to speak as a punishment, or as a detested animal, such as a dog or a snake. Alternatively, his next life will be beset with mishaps.

2.

The Meaning and Purpose of Reincarnation Therapy

In those countries where belief in reincarnation is an everyday matter, very much more harmony may be observed in the mentality of the people. Life is seen as being surrounded by eternity and not as a short span with a sudden beginning and a sudden ending. Therefore many fears, problems and tensions, typical in western countries, do not arise at all: dependence on material wealth and external security; fear of loss, fear of the future, fear of death, restless behaviour and being pressed for time, lack of flexibility and over-reaction to disappointment. If life is seen as a river which may go through various stages, but never ceases to flow, then you are unlikely to develop an exaggerated dependence on material objects. You know that you have already possessed many things and left them behind. Neither are you likely to become dependent on a loved one and worry about losing him or her, if you know that you have already been with that same person, sometimes in several lives and that you will perhaps meet him or her again in a later life – if fate wills it. Death has nothing in itself to make you frightened, it merely indicates that the present level of consciousness is over and must make way for the next one and even an early death has its justification in the fate of the individual.

Reincarnation therapy, like every other form of psychology, has the aim of making unconscious areas conscious and therefore harmless. As soon as the origin of a problem has been found and worked through, that problem can be solved. If the origin of a conflict lies in childhood, then a therapy session where childhood is discussed should solve the problem. If the origin of some wrong development was in the antenatal period, during a phase in pregnancy or during the birth itself, then a reliving of the antenatal period will solve the problem. However if the origin of the problem lies in earlier lives, then it is only reincarnation therapy which can solve this problem. This means that it is important to choose the right form of therapy. If a problem lies in former lives and the origin is sought in the childhood of this life, one can carry on for years with therapy which is more or less useless. In the same way if a situation of conflict lies in the present, reincarnation therapy will not bring any relief. Most chronic problems do, however, have their origin in earlier lives. Two children, growing up in the same parental home, may develop entirely different reactions to their parents and to their surroundings and may have entirely different problems. It is not that our environment imprints itself on us, but rather that it activates those tendencies in us which we have already brought with us.

In reincarnation therapy, ancient wisdom and philosophy combine in an ideal way with modern psychological technology. Through the support of modern psychology, philosophy receives concrete confirmation and through integration with philosophy, psychology is considerably enriched. Psychology should really be an applied philosophy, bringing a person more consciousness, balance and understanding. This is realised in reincarnation therapy, which regards present reactions and problems as the remains of a past reality which are imprinting themselves on our present outlook on life. Present opinions and ideas often stem from former painful experiences and if these experiences can be fundamentally worked through and the pain contained in them released, a person's whole picture of the world can be altered.

I would like to illustrate this with an actual case: One day a young woman came to the practice. Her dark eyes gave the impression of being uneasy and rather nervous. Ever since she was four years old she had been subject to attacks of asthma. During these attacks she became overheated, her clothing suddenly felt too tight and uncomfortable, and she could not bear to be touched by other people.

This young woman, whom we will call Erika, had in her present real life not managed to separate herself from the parental home. This is an important point, which is seen again and again in asthma sufferers. As a grown woman she was still experiencing an over-anxious mother and a strongly authoritative father. She was not able to assert herself much in life and so it came about that she was always browbeaten, in both her professional and personal life. She reacted against this by coming out in skin rashes.

Her first reincarnation session provided the following picture. In deep relaxation Erika 'sees' a caravan in the desert. The travelling party is on its way to a town, intending to buy for the young woman everything necessary for her wedding, her trousseau and dowry. The wedding is to be soon. The young nineteen-year-old woman is dressed as a rich bedouin girl, curly black hair peeping out from under her veil. Only her merry, black eyes are to be seen, all the rest of her face is veiled. She is looking forward to seeing the town. 'A change at last', she thinks and shakes off the memory of her life in the desert tents. There she had no say in things, no decisions to make, she had to serve and wait on the men. Suddenly there comes a sandstorm. The sky becomes black. They have to dismount from the camels. The beasts seek shelter behind the shifting dunes. The girl presses close up against her camel, burying her head in her arms in protection. The hot wind blows over her, hot grains of sand penetrate into her mouth, her nose and her burning eyes; there is very little shelter. Soon her head and her body are both covered in sand. She tries to stand up, but it is impossible. In despair she clings tightly to the camel, feeling rising terror. She tries to scream, but as soon as she opens her mouth it is filled with more sand. The camel becomes uneasy and gets up jerkily and now this protection has gone too. More and more sand piles up over her head and body. She has no more air, fear rises to panic, the hot sand seems to be forcing its way into her lungs. The storm abates only gradually. She tries to drag herself along, her body is hot and exhausted. She cannot find out anything about her travelling companions. There is not a human soul, not a camel, nothing at all. Only hot sand and the merciless sun which has risen in the meantime. Everything hurts, her eyes burn, her throat is dry, parched with thirst. She feels that she is going to have to die. The first vultures appear in the sky. The first blisters are appearing on her skin. She becomes unconscious. Presently she dies. . . When the young woman was reliving this past life in the desert, she found it dull. From her present point of view she could see that she was nothing more than a chattel because she was going to be sold to her bridegroom.

There are several parallels with her present life. When her parents allowed it she liked travelling, and when free of her parents' care she was enterprising. Just as in her former life, when she left the wilderness and the boredom and was off to an independent life, she was full of liveliness. But this apparent independence also showed her dependence on her parents: as soon as she went on her travels alone, the asthma attacks became more frequent. Even harmless sneezing could bring on lack of air. This was followed by a dry, troublesome cough. Her throat became dry (as in the desert). In crowded rooms she became claustrophobic. On her travels she was seized by a restless feeling of expectancy – she thought she might be missing something. A lot of birds in the sky frightened her. Where men were concerned, she felt that as a woman she was being repressed, she was not appreciated enough, she thought men had more advantages than women.

In a further reincarnation session she experienced the following picture: 'I see a medieval market place, I am standing on a platform, I am about thirty-five years old. I am tied up in some way, I cannot move my arms or my legs either. In front of me there is a shouting, roaring crowd of people. Some of them are angry, others are laughing in an ugly way. Shouts of "blasphemer, witch" comes ringing up to me. Diagonally a little to my left there is a man, you can't recognise his face, he has a white hood drawn up over his head. In front of him there is a barrel on a fire. Something is boiling and bubbling inside it. There is a stink of hot tar. The executioner goes to the barrel with a big ladle and ladles out some of the bubbling hot stuff. he comes to me . . . no, not that! No, please don't!' . . . She is breathing heavily, she starts back in terror and pain. When she calms down, she blurts out jerkily, 'He poured it over my shoulders. Hazily I am aware of the yelling crowd below me. The man with the hot ladle keeps coming back and back. I try to avoid the deadly stuff by twisting my body about, but it is no good.'

She begins breathing painfully and has to take a deep breath before she can go on speaking. 'The people are spurring the torturer on. I feel myself beginning to fight against a feeling of faintness. Why are these people doing this? After all, I am not guilty. I have never done anything to anyone. I only wanted to help, I saved the child, the mother died in childbirth, how can I help it?'

'They could have forgiven her about the child, but not her affair with a married man. He had been her great love. How could she have suspected that he had been the one who had handed her over to the Inquisition? He wanted to save his marriage and the money his wife possessed, he wanted to be able to go on living a comfortable life. Soldiers had taken her away and she had had to spend three days in a dungeon underground. The priest they sent her said she must expiate her sin, she was a blasphemer.'

Just as in the example in the desert, we have here a connection with her present life: sensitive skin, burning eyes, shortness of breath, an exaggerated sense of shame in relation to men. She feels herself 'injured' by men and behaves very cautiously where they are concerned.

3.

Trauma from the Womb

Each course of reincarnation therapy begins with a preliminary talk from which I obtain a picture of the life situation of the person who has come to me. Important points are the experience of childhood and relationship with parents, brothers and sisters. Conflicts and difficulties already apparent in childhood are clear pointers to earlier lives, these difficulties being both of an inner nature, such as taking offence easily, shyness or aggression, and of an external nature, such as the loss of a parent, the effects of war or other tragic circumstances. In reincarnation therapy we proceed from the assumption that a person's present childhood is a continuation of his former lives. Anything which has not been worked through will be encountered again in childhood.

Operations and accidents are important. Since every word and phrase uttered by doctors or medical staff during anaesthesia penetrates unfiltered into the subconscious and may act as a suggestion, this suggestive material must in some cases first be made conscious before regression into former lives can begin. Such a suggestive sentence as 'It is all in vain', or 'We are not making any progress', for example, can give the client the feeling in every session that there is no point in the therapy and that he is not going to make any progress. It is not until these blocks have been removed that an unhindered entry into the subconscious will be possible.

The relationship with the marriage partner and with the opposite sex in general also gives information about the makeup of the client's personality and about possible problems which may arise. There are some people whose every relationship with a partner ends in the same way, wrecked by the same problems. In this case the person has a problem which has not been worked out and which keeps producing similar forms of expression again and again in the partnership. When a certain type of person is chosen again and again as a partner, this is another indication of the client's makeup. For example, if a woman always has authoritative partners, who want to rule her life, the reincarnation therapist knows that unconsciously she always attracts the same situation in order to work something out in it, in order to learn something from it. Since most situations repeated in the present bear the stamp of past lives, one could in this case trace back the theme of 'authority being ruled and ruling'.

Losses which are hard to bear, such as the death of a fellow human being or a separation, are an indication that in former lives this person suffered heavy losses. They recur when similar circumstances arise in the present life making the loss appear even more painful.

All the things which a person encounters continually in his present life and which he finds hard to bear, which create problems for him and depress his morale, are signs of past experiences which have not been worked out.

During this first conversation and also during regressions, my clients are connected up to a so-called biofeedback apparatus, whose needle unerringly indicates those points containing traumatic material. Life usually begins and ends with trauma – this is an expression of the conflict between the soul and the physical plane. Physical life begins with conception. The constellation of the heavens at conception, as well as the inward attitude of the parents during conception, have a direct correspondence with the soul of the child. Since the soul comes into the world and is incarnated here in order to solve previous problems, it is attracted by parents who have a problem similar to its own. This problem shared by the parents and the child is already present at conception. The external circumstance of conception, pregnancy and birth are a reflection of the inner situation of the child. A great deal of research has recently been published on this subject; for example the great effect which the experience of the mother during pregnancy has on the feelings and the emotional world of the child. However, the true beginning of this analogy is to be found in the child's choice of its parents before conception. Since in the preparatory sessions of reincarnation therapy, birth and the prenatal phase are worked on first, enough material could be collected here for a comparison of the tendencies which the child brings with it and its choice of parents. Important points which make this clearer are: the thoughts and feelings of the parents during conception;

the first reaction of the mother or father to the pregnancy; the way the mother or father copes with pregnancy; whether the child is wanted or not; what is expected of the child; the behaviour of the parents to one another during pregnancy; the parents' problems during pregnancy (which need not necessarily be concerned only with the health problems of the mother or father during pregnancy itself); deep seated fears, especially those of the mother; deeply felt losses (as, for example, the loss of someone who is close) and finally, the course of the birth itself. All the typical problems which a person has in his life as well as many health disorders have their origin in the prenatal phase and in the birth. Here are a few examples to illustrate this.

After the death of her husband, Helga suffered from considerable fears extending into all aspects of her life; for example fear of being alone, fear of death, fear of heat, fear of overcrowded, confined rooms to name but a few. She always sought support from others and expected them to protect her. After the death of her husband this expectation was directed towards her children and the neighbours. During the prenatal phase of this client the following information came to light.

The mother was half-Jewish and during the Third Reich she got to know a man who was not a Jew. She hoped to become pregnant by him, so that he would marry her and she would thus become safe from being persecuted as a Jew. Her first reaction when the doctor confirmed her pregnancy was 'Thank God, now I am safe', but then doubt set in: 'What will become of me and the baby? Will it save me from the Concentration Camp? I hope Karl (the father) will stay beside me. Will he be able to protect me when I need him?'

During the whole pregnancy the mother was very much afraid that something might go wrong, that she would be betrayed and would have to go away after all. At birth the child suffered acute claustrophobia; she felt pressure on all sides, which particularly affected her head and shoulders. She felt nervous because she had to get out, she felt she was being torn apart. In this case the woman was born into a war situation strongly marked by fear for her life and future, also by hope and at the same time great uncertainty. Just as her mother wanted to be protected, so my client also wanted to be protected. The fears remained latent as long as my client was protected in life, but after the death of her husband, the fear of being left alone and with it all the other fears surfaced in her consciousness. When these original situations in her prenatal phase were relived, the fear was considerably lessened.

The next case concerns a young woman named Renate, who on the one hand suffered from feelings of inferiority and deep vulnerability, but on the other hand was herself very cold and offensive and often told lies about other people for material profit. At worst she resorted to blackmail and suicide threats in order to achieve her purpose. This dichotomy led to a permanent state of anxiety with depressions, which this woman sought to cure with tablets.

When my client's mother became pregnant her first reaction to the coming baby had been: 'Now I have someone of my own'.

The following dialogue took place between the parents: Her father: 'Must it happen' (roughly). My client's mother cried, thinking: 'There is no sense in bringing a child into the world to be with this man. He is behaving as if I could do something about it'. Her father: 'Well, then, we shall just have to get married.' My client's mother feels that her lover is not doing this because of any real affection for her, but only from a sense of duty. But, since she wants to have a father for the child, she agrees.

Conception had taken place after a quarrel between the parents-to-be. The woman had seen her lover with another woman and had been jealous. During intercourse, she was thinking: 'If something happens now, he will leave that other woman. He will have to make it up to me for being faithful to him, when he has not been faithful to me.'

She has feelings of revenge and at the same time feels her own worthlessness. 'I do so much for him and yet he goes to that other woman.'

During intercourse, the man is thinking: 'She would really be a model wife, a good housewife, but the other one is good for sex.'

After a later quarrel, when her time is getting on, my client's mother wants to pay her husband back and tries to get rid of the baby by means of hip-baths. When the jet of water is turned on, the unborn child feels as if she were being pierced through. Her head aches and she thinks: 'Just leave me in peace'.

The attempted abortion is a failure.

At the birth, the mother is given an anaesthetic, which also affects the child. The child becomes unconscious and knows nothing about the whole birth. The behavioural pattern of revenge as compensation for weakness and paying off the partner is clearly shown by both parents. During a private talk, the client's mother was able to confirm these prenatal occurrences. Immediately after the session about what happened before she was born, there was a marked improvement in the client's general condition.

Reliving what happened before birth often brings to light things which the client did not know before. These may be family secrets which the child was never supposed to know, for example that the baby was to be given away for adoption, or that the father was not the real father. If one of the parents dies very early and the child no longer has any conscious memory of him or her, the client will get to know the parent while reliving the pregnancy, as in the following case: Cecily, who is forty years old, never knew her father because he died when she was four. She herself had a problem with her partner, which resulted in a power struggle.

At conception her mother remains passive, she would like to withdraw from her husband although she is devoted to him, because she is afraid of becoming pregnant. She thinks, 'I can't take on this responsibility, but yet I can't oppose him, I must submit to him.' Her father is overcome by feelings for her mother, he calms her down, saying 'Nothing is going to happen, I would like to be with you always'.

At this moment the client was overcome by the feeling of being able to imagine her father properly for the first time, how he was as a person, and she felt very close to him. She had always respected him very much, although she had not known him.

Later her mother blamed her father: 'It is your fault that I am pregnant, you forced me.' Her father is shocked and declares that he loves her. Her mother cries, she feels that she has wounded him. Here the unborn child feels shocked. 'My mother is putting my life in question, she is only agreeing to me with reservations, I won't stay here. I want to get out quickly.' (The baby was, indeed, premature.) In the third month the baby senses that someone else is there. 'There is something hard there like me, it is irritating me and amusing me, I am curious about it, we smile at each other, then there is not enough room, it is a squash, but it's nice and cosy, we try to share the room.'

(Here the client was experiencing her twin sister). When the waters burst during the birth, the baby got a pain in the heart, 'my head is bursting, I am suffocating, coughing, thrashing about.' After this premature birth, the babies were so weak that they had an emergency baptism because people were afraid that they were going to die. The client felt that she was not accepted in her mother's womb, and this became a pattern in her life. She often (quickly) felt herself rejected; on the other hand she liked to offer resistance, as her mother had done to her father. If one of the parents does not accept the child during pregnancy, then a rejection problem will probably arise in the life of the child. Later it always secretly feels rejected, however much everyone round it praises it and shows affection towards it, it simply cannot believe them. The choking feeling in the throat, together with difficulty in breathing, as at birth, were accompanying symptoms of painful situations in the later life of this client.

The experiences of twins in the womb are not always so positive as in the case just mentioned. Often souls which have been enemies before meet again as twins.

When Helmut experienced in the womb that there was another baby there, he reacted in the following way: 'For goodness sake, not again! We meet again now, I feel disturbed. When we get bigger, there is tension. I push him to the wall, I do not take any notice of him, I am entirely self-centred, my brother is just a shadow.'

Helmut also experienced his own fertilization. 'Funnel-shaped threads are running together, I see egg cells and seeds melting into one another, I am concentrating all my attention on it, I am enveloped in something grey-white. It is pleasant. . .' The client's parents did not agree about the pregnancy. His mother's first reaction to the pregnancy was: 'This time I really would like to have the baby, last time I had an abortion. This time I will not stand for that from my husband.' His father reacted to the pregnancy in this way: 'It's quite out of the question that we should have a child.' the mother said defiantly, 'Yes, we will. You must finally take the responsibility. I want to have the baby.' The father: 'Is it really mine?' The mother: 'Certainly it is.'

The client's birth experience involves great fear, his body is seized by a strong vibration, he has a feeling of mountain sickness. At the birth the mother does not push enough and the baby has great difficulty in getting through the birth canal. Difficulty in breathing and deadly fear arise. When the baby is finally out, it feels very much alone and forsaken, it does not feel any relationship with its mother. 'Nobody loves me, I am sad as though I know that a lot of hardship is coming to me in life. I feel hatred towards my brother; pay attention to me! I am the elder! My parents are friendlier towards him, I have to take notice of him now.'

This client had a great problem in his life with being recognised and he made great efforts to be loved and recognised by those around him. Later too his relationship with his twin brother was very tense, his parents liked his twin brother better and often held him up as an example, which increased his secretly rising hatred. His twin brother died at an early age, of cancer. During regression into former lives it emerged that these two brothers had done a lot of harm to each other.

Eric often found himself unwanted and pushed into the background in life. He had the feeling of being inadequate. He also had a time problem in the form of a fear of being too late and an anxiety about appointments, which had to be kept.

His mother reacted uneasily to the pregnancy. 'I don't want to be pregnant, he doesn't want any children just at this time, when everything is uncertain (Wartime). Who knows whether he will come back, whether it will be all right, we have had so little time to ourselves.' The baby feels itself unwelcome here. 'I feel guilty, I'm making trouble; I would like you to like me, I'm so helpless myself.' His mother thinks: 'I'm not so sure about my relationship with my husband, whether he is not just staying with me out of a sense of duty, he took a long time deciding on me, I'm not really worth much.' The baby thinks: 'Just give me a little time, I'll be quite quiet, then I shall be the least trouble.'

Children sometimes have feelings of guilt when they come at an awkward time for their parents and they unconsciously make promises to make it up to the parents if only they will keep them and accept them. The mother feels worthless because her husband did not marry her for herself and the baby feels worthless because it appeared too early and was not welcome. This client's two problems of worth and time are obviously contained in the prenatal phase.

When we begin the therapy with the antenatal period, we encourage the client with words like these: 'We are now going into the prenatal phase of the pregnancy. You are already there. You are in the womb. Give the number of any month in the pregnancy from 1 to 9, whichever comes into your head first.'

That is the starting point. Now come the first indications and immediately I go on to ask 'If your mother has a problem in this month of her pregnancy, what is it? Tell me word for word what she is thinking in this month.'

As a rule I immediately get answers about that time. The child is not yet able to think, but the subconscious contains the stored-up thoughts of that period.

The mother's and father's problems of that time recur in the child's thoughts. What chiefly concerned its mother and father during the pregnancy will recur in a similar way in the child's life.

The father's and mother's problems will be worked through by defining them in this way: 'What difficulties did your mother have during her pregnancy, what worried her? Let your mother say in her own words what she is thinking at such a moment.'

Naturally the problems and thoughts of the mother are rather nearer to the child than those of the father, because the child is always close to the mother, but only experiences the father from time to time.

If one parent rejects the pregnancy and the other wants it very much, the child can ally itself with the parent who is in favour of the pregnancy and make promises to this parent, such as: 'I will always help you', 'I will never be a burden to you', 'I will protect you and do everything for you.' As soon as it is a question of the pregnancy being rejected, the therapist will look out for promises such as the child is making here. This can lead in later life to a more difficult separation from this parent, since the child feels that it should not break its promise now by going away.

'What misgivings has your mother/father got about the pregnancy?'

'Are there any fears on the part of your mother or your father?'

Even when a child is wanted, the parents may have some misgivings. This is perfectly natural, but they will have gone into the child's subconscious and should be brought to light in order not to influence the child any further.

We work through the pregnancy back to conception, which is the first concrete life situation connecting the incarnating soul with its new body. Already it reflects the child's life work. The thoughts, attitudes and feelings of the parents towards one another do stamp their character on the course of the child's life, although the child has already established a tendency in that direction. Thus, the child's reaction to what happens during pregnancy will vary according to its nature: a soul which is uncertain and possessed by fear may take all the blame for the parents' rejection and feel itself repressed and disconcerted. In later life it may react in a very susceptible way to rejection, whereas a more belligerent soul might say in a similar case, 'Here goes. I will win through and not let myself be put off.' In neither case are the parents in any way to blame for not behaving properly during pregnancy or for influencing their child in a negative way with negative thoughts, since, after all, it always comes down to what the child itself makes of the situations before its birth.

The birth is worked through stage by stage. I ask particularly about physical impressions, since the actual delivery is difficult and often dangerous. The birth itself can leave its imprint on later problems and conflicts. Most of my clients report physical stress to the point of actual pain, with me insisting: Describe this pain, this stress. Where exactly do you feel it? What do you actually experience? What are your feelings at that time?'

Often what is felt is pressure in the head, squeezing in the region of the neck and shoulders, lack of breath with fear of suffocation and the feeling that one is not going to make it and is going to die during birth. During the actual regression, unpleasant physical sensations such as pressure in the head or a feeling of constriction may set in but disappear again later. I take care not to let my client go through the birth too quickly without coming into contact with pain. Many clients are unwilling to recall unpleasant physical sensations and reach the end very quickly with the words: 'I am out already.'

Even a comparatively quick and uncomplicated birth is very trying for the baby and this first struggle in the child's life should be clearly experienced again in regression. It may happen that the client says: 'I can't feel my mother any more, she is no longer helping me, I am all alone, left in the lurch.' There is always a reason for feelings like these. It may be that here the mother, through exhaustion or resignation, has given up cooperating and pushing, or else she has been anaesthetized. The child then has the impression of being all alone and of having to work its way out alone; but birth should be a team effort between the mother and the child. There are children, too, who oppose being born and block the birth by not helping, but rather struggling against it. This makes the delivery very much harder for the mother. A further important phenomenon is the caesarian section, where the child does not have to fight its own way out, but is suddenly brought out by surgical intervention. One might think that this would be pleasant for the child, but in practice it appears that this intervention can be threatening for it. Thus one client was terrified when she saw the scalpel directed towards her mother and cried out: 'My God, what are they doing to my mother?' She was afraid they were going to kill her mother. Also, being pulled out suddenly and quickly gives the child no time to adjust to the outside world. People born in this way behave later in a very passive way and expect everything will be taken away from them by those around them, or else they become hyperactive, because they are living with the unconscious feeling of always having to fight for things, having to work for something which eluded them at birth.

As soon as the birth is over, I ask about the first impressions of life. The atmosphere in the labour ward or at home in the bedroom, the first physical sensations, the first contacts with the staff, with its mother and father impress themselves strongly on the child. The bright lights and the coldness of the labour ward are unpleasant for the child; sudden movements, like being held up by the feet or being smacked on the back or on the bottom or being put on cold scales are annoying. Soon, too, hunger sets in. The child's body must now adapt to taking in nourishment by mouth and it takes some time before the child becomes accustomed to the new conditions of life.

The most important fact when I am working in the prenatal phase is this: the foetus does not possess any analytical consciousness, it cannot think independently. During the nine months, the foetus behaves like an unconscious tape recorder. The mother lives a conscious life, she eats, sleeps, thinks, speaks and feels and thus forms the conscious part of the unconscious foetus. Therefore when I am working in the antenatal phase, I do not allow my client to think that the data are his own data. They come from his mother or from the world around him. If during pregnancy the mother thinks, 'I can't bear it any longer' meaning the heat or the hard work, the unconscious recording apparatus of the foetus activates every experience from former lives and applies these thoughts of the mother to itself. I have known people to repeat whole conversations, without knowing where those conversations came from. I have known people say to me in Spanish or Italian things which were said to their mothers during pregnancy. They have not understood the meaning of these words nor have they heard them anywhere else.

Next I would like to relieve you of a possible worry. In this method of therapy, the conscious part of the client is never switched off. I do not use any kind of hypnotic suggestion. I never alter the consciousness of the person with whom I am working. A kind of hypnosis always does take place when one is working with human consciousness, only we allow our client to hypnotise himself to the degree which is necessary for him. He can place himself under hypnosis and remove the hypnosis again as required.

In reality by using this method we abolish hypnosis. We annul post-hypnotic suggestions, when we go back hundreds and thousands of years. One of the greatest problems of every therapy except this one, is the block caused by birth. Whenever a drug is introduced into the body, which alters conscious perception, an incomplete experience will result. Sooner or later one will have to go back and go through the experience to the end. In this therapy a client will sometimes find it difficult to decide whether he is the mother or the child, the doctor or the nurse or someone altogether different. When this happens I must take care that he remains inside his body, he must never lose contact with his body.

During the process of birth, when the mother is under an anaesthetic, the doctors and midwives will very often say something like this: 'She is unconscious now', 'She can't hear anything', 'She doesn't know what is happening'. However, when patients come to report such sentences, they will say, 'I can't hear anything', 'There is nothing there', 'I can't see anything'. At such moments they are merely reproducing what has been said around them, not their own experiences. If I do not recognise this, then precisely the material which has caused his problem will be excluded and an empty space will be created, which leads to nothing further. However, as soon as one begins to work with a patient on an unconscious level, he will immediately penetrate into that empty space, where he cannot see or hear anything.

We now try to find out what is the cause of this empty space.

You may ask: 'When the doctor says words which cause this feeling in you, where would the doctor be standing, on the right or on the left, at the head of the bed or at the foot?' The patient must concentrate on just this one question. I do not allow him to go any further. As soon as the patient has fixed the position of the doctor, he can become aware that he is listening to what someone else is saying.

We all recognise in ourselves and in our patients behavioural patterns which avoid everything, hinder everything, cause us always to be prejudiced against something. Such behaviour derives chiefly from birth, when the child could not be born easily. Birth lays down the pattern of how the person will deal with stress in later life, because birth is the first experience of stress in this life.

You should know that during birth extraneous things may be present, for example words may be called out in the next room, which the foetus notes without realising that these words are not its own. I have worked with patients who were firmly convinced that they themselves and their mother died during the birth and in some miraculous way went on living afterwards. While working it through, we found that someone beside them had died or that the doctors had been talking to each other about a dying patient.

For this reason I can only stress that especially at the time of birth every problem which a patient has is firmly established in word and deed. Acceptance of this fact has always led to success. In this connection, it may be birth in the present life or in a former one. If I find it is a former birth them similar material must exist in the present one too, and both must be worked through.

Work with birth leads to all kinds of discoveries. A patient may say: 'This woman is not my mother,' and a dialogue comes to light on the subject of having the baby adopted. The patient realises for the first time that he was adopted. One can find out other things too, which will be a shock to the patient, for example, that the man who brought the patient up is not his real father or that his mother was not always faithful. All these dynamic discoveries will have an influence on the patient. Often the prenatal phase or the birth itself will contain some sort of secret, which the patient does not consciously know, but yet he has the feeling of having to keep something hushed up.

Many sexual problems derive from the period before birth, especially up to the fifth or sixth month. If it is a male foetus and the mother, because of her discomfort in the sex act, thinks: 'I wish he would hurry up and get it over,' it is not difficult to imagine that the foetus in question will, as a grown man, suffer from premature ejaculation. On the other hand, if it is a female foetus and the mother thinks in the sex act: 'Is it never going to stop, I can't bear it any longer,' this child may later have difficulties with orgasm. What is said during the prenatal phase is of utmost importance for the baby. And it is not only the words spoken – the thoughts of the mother will become the baby's thoughts.

In many philosophies the existence of pain is denied: 'Pain does not really exist, but rather one is in disharmony with what is experiencing pain'. During therapy, when a patient is reporting about his mother and reproduces her thoughts as follows: 'Everything is fine, splended, I love my husband, I am glad that I am pregnant,' these are thoughts which touch only on the surface. When I reach the prenatal phase and nothing comes to light: 'Everything is fine,' then I ask: 'Please go below the surface in your mother's thoughts and tell me the first words your mother is *thinking*, not saying.'

There are three periods in the prenatal phase. It is not necessary to go fully into all three, but in order to make it clearer I have divided them up as follows:

First period: conception up to the point where the pregnancy is officially confirmed. The mother may suspect that she is pregnant, she may or may not hope that she is pregnant, but the pregnancy has not yet been confirmed. For this reason the baby is not yet the centre of attention and therefore it is at this point still very vulnerable. At this time the mother may still do a lot of things which she would not do if she knew that she was pregnant, for example riding on a roller coaster.

When the pregnancy is confirmed the mother's first reaction is important, it will lay down a pattern for the baby. If the mother's first reaction is: 'Oh God, no!' we shall discover rejection or fear of being rejected as a fundamental behavioural pattern in the patient. The mother may indeed immediately after her first reaction say: 'It is all right, we want a child anyway,' but now we have as behavioural pattern: 'reject me/ love me'. Here we find a person who right at the beginning of a relationship with someone else is looking for ways to make the other person reject them. At the same time they are very much afraid of being rejected. Such people spend their lives either hopelessly alone or in relationships in which they are rejected.

It is a great mistake to let people think that they are being rejected, since someone with this behavioural pattern will always find ways and means of being rejected, no matter what is going on around them. You can say to them 'I love you' and they will say 'Yes, but you have not said it often enough, you have not said it loudly enough.'

From just these nine months of the prenatal phase we can discover all the patient's problems and behavioural patterns, which he will repeat again and again in his life. I teach new reincarnation therapists to work in this area and to leave past lives alone. Previous lives can be gone into after the prenatal phase.

The second period of the prenatal phase is the time from the beginning of pregnancy up to the seventh month. In my work I have often found traumata in this phase. When I was talking to a doctor about this, I found out that it is precisely in the seventh month that the formative phase of the brain is completed and the baby becomes physically more aware. Patients sometimes say: 'My mother would never say such a thing, never do such a thing', but, believe me, one can never know what a mother may or may not do during pregnancy.

Often one has to overcome the fear of finding out something which the client should not know about his parents. Of course it is just the things which the client already knows, but ought not to know, which give rise to problems. During this second period everything positive and negative revolves round the baby. This phase has a great influence on the child.

When there are problems about weight, one can hear the mother, in the sixth month, saying, 'I'm getting so heavy, I'm getting so fat, I can't move'.

We always have to listen carefully to the patient. If his problems seem like the problems of a pregnant woman, we know that they are not his problems, but they come from the prenatal phase.

The third period from the seventh month until birth is often a source of depression. People in a depression often use expressions coming from the last two and a half months before birth. Here are found blocks and unconscious orders. 'I am so tired, I can't move, I would really like just to go on lying in bed.' These are all things which would be said by a woman in the eighth month, not by the person in front of us. Depressive people often do not want to give up their depression, since they are afraid of taking this step, because it is when the depression recedes that the real therapy begins. Often the mother will have tried to put off the birth because she was afraid. If she is given drugs at the birth, this will end in suppressed depression. So fear ends in depression and this is the way one will behave in life: if ever one senses fear, one will be depressed because that was the way it ended in the prenatal phase. Now and then a nervous woman will get into a panic over labour pains and become hysterical if she then receives medication to make her unconscious. We have hysteria = manic phase, and drugs = depressive phase, ie manic depression. The experience in labour will be re-activated by stress in later life and so the patient's behaviour in life will be manic, then depressive, manic and again depressive and so on.

When these manic-depressive people go to the doctor to have sedatives prescribed, they are, thereby, duplicating exactly the birth experience. Fear is followed by drugs and this leads to depression.

Patients sometimes ask their mother: 'What was it like when I was born?' 'Oh, it was very easy, you were a wanted child, I just went into the hospital and had you.'

When I work through this birth, I find that the mother screamed terribly and real horror stories emerge. But mothers tend to block out the memory of labour pains. The pain lies deeper. Many men have this picture of a painless birth, because they have never given birth themselves in this life. I do not believe, 'there is no pain.' I work through the birth all the same, because perhaps there is no pain only because someone says there is none and suppresses it.

One of the most serious birth experiences I ever worked through appeared at the beginning to be just a simple birth. At the end of the delivery, the doctor said: 'It is a good thing she was unconscious and she will never find out what really happened here.'

It took five hours to go through this birth, when normally I need only half an hour. The doctor's words suppressed the experience, 'Nothing happened.'

When a mother goes fully conscious into the labour ward, is conscious of the pains and experiences the delivery without anything to deaden the pain, then that experience is over and done with. It is not necessarily transmitted to the child. However a mother is often unprepared both mentally and physically for the birth. She has no idea what is awaiting her and then she screams: 'I can't bear it any longer, is it never going to end.' Therefore the experience of pain never does end. If there were some way of stopping anything being said during labour, the child would never know that there was any pain there. The theory is that whenever consciousness is not present, everything around a person will take the place of consciousness.

The phase immediately after birth is also very vulnerable. Every word spoken after birtth up to the age of three years, has great significance and influences what the child will do one day. If a child is ill-treated up to the age of five or six years, this will have a devastating effect on that child's later life.

I once had a patient who was weeping aloud in the waiting room. She said the pain was so great that she could not bear it any longer. I knew that she was reliving her birth, but she insisted that she was crying because her friend had left her. I regressed her to her birth, although she kept repeating: 'The pain is so great, I cannot bear it', 'I am going to die.' She accepted the fact that she was reliving her birth only when she repeated to me the words of the doctor.

This is an example of how one can deduce from hearing only a couple of sentences that a patient is reliving the birth experience. She said to me: 'Be quiet, I won't do it.' I said that these were her mother's words to the doctor. She would not accept this, until she heard the doctor say 'Push, push!'

Whatever pain a patient may suffer from will be found at his birth. If someone has a particular pain, eg in the back, I only have to ask when dealing with his birth, 'What produced a pain in the back in this birth?' and the patient will tell me.

Work in the field of reincarnation therapy is divided into three sections: 1) Present life back to birth. 2) From birth back to conception. 3) Time before conception.

It does not matter whether we call this time visualisation, imagination, fantasy or former lives. All that matters is the success we can achieve by working in this area.

4.

Death and Karma

Birth and death remind people of the eternally moving process of dying and becoming, of the ceaseless flow of life energy. Babies are regarded with astonishment and awe; death makes us reflective; sometimes it alarms us and challenges us to ponder on the sense of life.

In reincarnation therapy we often concern ourselves with death experiences from former lives, because many fears such as bodily suffering, many firm opinions and convictions have become deeply imprinted on our unconscious for the very reason that death put its stamp on them in a former life. In previous lives we did not always die a natural death; often our death was violent and sudden, and this administered a shock to mind and body.

In moments of acute mortal danger, values and time may alter; then may be a sudden flash of insight which would never have occurred in our day-to-day consciousness. In the light of this insight, the soul tries to formulate a solution, in order to avoid such dangers in the future. This solution, which is tailor-made for that specific situation, is later used by the person for other situations which it does not fit. Each situation in life happens once only and should always be considered and solved for that moment alone. Therefore 'preconceived' solutions do not fit new situations and they introduce problems of their own.

Let us assume that a woman was killed in a former life by being stabbed in the heart with a dagger by her husband because he wanted to take possession of her property. This woman was taken completely by surprise by this gruesome side of her husband and may have thought just before her death: 'I would never have thought it of him, the scoundrel. Men are false and treacherous, you can't ever trust any of them.' In this conviction, this woman's life came to an end and the conviction has accompanied her into her next life, where she now treats every man with suspicion and is afraid of marriage. In situations of stress, pains in the heart may occur; in financial affairs she may be of the opinion that it is better to give money away and not accumulate too many possessions. She may be very cautious towards life in general and always have the feeling that some accident may bring her life to an untimely end. Everything leading to an unnatural death is stored up most minutely in her subconscious. If in her former life her husband had merely seized her fortune and sent her away, the whole event would not have penetrated so deeply, but everything leading to an unnatural death or any contributing circumstance gains increased importance.

If a woman was burnt at the stake during the Middle Ages, because she had had unlawful relations with a man, not only will death by burning be recorded in her subconscious, perhaps reappearing as fear of fire or as skin disease in a later life, but also the whole problem of human relationships and the morals of this period may later come to the surface. This woman may in a later life be extremely cautious about relationships, she may set great store by legal contracts and be afraid of lighthearted adventures – or else out of a certain kind of defiance, she may give herself over entirely to illicit relationships in order, subconsciously, to bring the previous unfinished relationship to a happier conclusion. In certain circumstances, she may throw herself compulsively into superficial relationships, in order to demonstrate that she will not allow herself to be put under pressure by any moral attitude and she may feel very happy in this role, since it means release from the previous compulsion. Of course this new behaviour is only a compensation for the previous uncompleted business and does not represent any real solution. But the soul often thinks that in order to solve a problem it need only do the opposite from what it did last time – thus giving rise to really contradictory 'schizophrenic' behaviour. If the original life situation, which was not worked out, is integrated in reincarnation therapy, then compensatory behaviour will not be necessary.

If a person was deliberately tortured, for example on the rack, the intense feeling of pain gives rise also to strong emotions, such as hate, revenge, anger, apathy and resignation. In such situations it is not surprising that the helpless victim will have such thoughts as: 'I will pay you back, if I catch one of you, I will do him in.' A person bringing such a burden with him will consider and treat those around him in his present life as his enemies and will, in some circumstances, be continually trying to do people a bad turn, and cause them injury. If a nice, pleasant life is brought to an end by an unnatural death, the person concerned will not be able to trust his luck in his next life and will adopt a pessimistic attitude towards it. He will unconsciously always be waiting for the calamity which must be coming soon and, therefore, he is never really willing to take on anything.

The departure of the soul from the body after a painful, traumatic death is always considered as a release. Physical consciousness recedes, the soul withdraws more and more from the body, until it has freed itself completely from it. It now looks down from above on the scene it has just left and is concerned. If, during his lifetime, a person has not concerned himself with life or death or life after death, he may be surprised in this situation to find that his consciousness still exists, although his body is lying lifeless below. This knowledge comes as a blow to suicides, who tried to avoid their problems by killing themselves and now find that after death these same problems are confronting them and will not go away.

After every death, the soul draws up a balance sheet of the life which has just ended. It subtracts what it has already dealt with and solved and it sorts out what still remains to be dealt with as an unfinished task. This task, this aim, now continues into the next incarnation. If someone has led a very selfish life and only used other people for his own purposes, his verdict after death may be: 'I must be less selfish and be more useful to other people.' After the new task has been formulated, the soul will wait for an incarnation which contains possibilities of achieving this aim.

One's own conscience can be suppressed during life, but after death it reappears and judges incorruptibly and clearly, according to the highest ethical principles, the life which has just ended.

There is no general rule as to how long the soul will remain between lives. It may be that suitable parents are available right away, in which case it may be drawn into a new body only seconds after the previous death. This sometimes happens after a sudden, dreadful death, but the soul may also remain for ages in the interim state. After the verdict has been given and the aim has been formulated, there is no further real progress on the other side. The soul may interchange with other souls, it may stay in pleasant spheres, but the learning of lessons must take place here on earth. That is why the soul must incarnate so often, until it has learnt all it has to learn.

Physical pain, shock, intense emotion, the sad loss of loved ones, of one's own life and being prevented by death from accomplishing important tasks as well as the remorseless balance sheet drawn up by one's own conscience after death – all these are reasons for a present fear of death. However, if one has in therapy worked through one's own former traumas, together with the accompanying experiences of death, then pain and death lose their terrors, because one becomes ever more conscious of one's own endless, indestructible being, one establishes a connection with that part of one's being which remains untouched by any outward event and this gives it a certainty and a security that no power in the world can take away from it.

Former traumas, former injuries, former feelings of guilt, former realisations of reality, especially childhood ones, but also the less tangible ones from a previous life, all these are stored up in our memory mechanism, in our subconscious and we let them all become superimposed on the consciousness of the moment. Anyone who insists on carrying the stones of the past around with him cannot hope to seize the chance of a new moment. The heavy stones of the past, which have become worthless, must be thrown away. We should do our best to begin by stripping them of all importance. In the end, because consciousness no longer charges them with energy, they shrivel up. They lose their weight and there is nothing left to carry round.

If this challenge is not met when a person faces death, this is for him only a postponement; what is not mastered in the present, becomes the life task of the next life.

When once one has recognised that this soul-spiritual development never ceases as long as difficulties in life remain to be overcome, and that one cannot escape from the problems but can only postpone them, one will adopt an ever calmer and more open attitude towards one's personal difficulties. Knowing that they will always be with us until we have resolved them – is it not really simpler to accept them at once and strive for a solution?

It is of course important to take the necessary lessons from the past – but we must not remain stuck in the past, we must go on further.

I have learnt a great deal from my work with sick people. If an illness takes a turn for the worse, then a transformation will appear. The obvious transformation facing this person is physical death. However a transformation may also take place here in life. If the transformation is understood rightly and if it is to be effective, then as complete a change in the attitude and in the pattern of life of the person concerned must take place as would take place as a result of death. Half measures are not sufficient here. There is no room for compromises. Comprehensive changes are necessary and everyone really knows which changes these must be. Summoning up the courage and the clarity to carry out the necessary changes — this is the real challenge. The predominant part of our ego puts off as long as possible any confrontation with illness and death.

Between birth and death there is a period in which both typical and individual development take place, the typical realm being humanity as a collective, the individual realm our personal biography. But does this apply only to our present life? For thousands of years the belief has persisted that man is not only born but born again; that our consciousness is not extinguished by death, but lives on at some time in another person; that our soul wanders through time and space instead of being extinguished or sleeping without memory through all eternity. Much can be explained as wishful thinking or pure imagination if not actual illusion, so caution is necessary, especially when dealing with such favourite characters for reincarnation as the pharaohs, Cleopatra or the priests of the temple, with whom many people like to identify themselves out of unsatisfied megalomania. Or particularly intense dreams may be taken for events which really happened in former lives. However, the wealth of material I have obtained, chiefly from my own experience, but also from the continual work of regressing others, is so varied and the evidence of the cases is too overwhelming for me to dismiss this phenomenon without commenting on it.

The reports given by serious medical men, by psychologists and parapsychologists on rebirth experiences are puzzling to many of us. The brain is often not able to grasp these things. Or do we perhaps know too little about it?

The famous American clairvoyant Edgar Cayce possessed strong mediumistic powers. When in the year 1901 he temporarily lost his senses and a doctor, who was unable to establish any pathalogical changes, treated him under hypnosis, unusual capacities came to light in Cayce. He fell into a light sleep, answered every question put to him and gave information which was astonishingly accurate. It was inexplicable where he had obtained knowledge of so many matters, knowledge which he could not have known in the normal way. It appeared as if in the trance condition he were connected up to a reservoir of knowledge and understanding, which remained closed to ordinary mortals. In the waking state he knew nothing at all about it.

However, for Cayce reincarnation became a key experience. Again and again when people, for whom he would give up all his spare time, came to him for advice, he would refer them to events and characters which made sense only in the context of a past life.

In 1927, when in a trance, he traced someone right back through history; he saw him as an attendant at the court of King Louis XIIIth of France, a few centuries earlier as an inhabitant of Salonika, before that in Persia, where the wandering soul was born again into the body of someone who became a doctor, further back to ancient Egypt 'at the time when the kingdom there was divided' and finally to legendary Atlantis, which is said to have sunk beneath the sea.

More than two thousand reports left behind by Cayce received special attention after his death and are still the subject of scientific interest today.

The impulse which drives a human being to go through one life cycle after another derives from the force of Karma. Physical actions, speech and mental actions create inward and outward experiences, which, in connection with the fruits of other deeds, become the origin of further and ever further fruits. Thus Karma leads to the combination of action and reaction extending from one life to another and determines the circumstances of each individual one. Belief in the knowledge of Karma should not be confused with any sort of Kismet fatalism. Even though we are bound to reap all that we sow, we are free to sow new seeds, which will yield good fruits. The consequences of Karma may be hard. For example a criminal suffers more than he would just through legal punishment or the fear of being found out. The consequences of his crime affect his personality.

Let us illustrate this with the example of a young teacher, who had ambivalent feelings towards his wife. One day he came to my practice reporting marital problems, saying that he felt under an obligation to his wife, and had difficulties with his parents-in-law, who would not accept him. He became aggressive when doubt was cast on his capabilities. In such situations he was provoked into showing his wife who was the stronger. Power struggles characterised the present marriage and the husband showed himself to be impulsive and domineering.

In a former life he had the experience of being a highwayman and robber. He seemed to recognise his wife and his parents-in-law from this life. Let us carefully examine the tape of his report:

'My men and I are holding up a coach. I am the leader, young, strong and proud. I am happy and it gives me deep satisfaction to hold up this coach. They are afraid of us and that pleases me. I turn to my men and call out arrogantly and insolently. I laugh and say: "Just look at them, those lords and masters!" We scare them out of their coach, an elderly couple and a very beautiful young girl. I see that she is eyeing me with concealed admiration. I pull her up on to my horse. We chase her two parents into the wood, just as though they were horses. My men fall upon the booty, but I am interested only in this girl with the red hair.'

After this event, he separates from his band. His life is changed. Till now, he has been the strong leader of the band, plundering rich people and appearing to his men as the strong man always ready for action. The influence of the red-haired Jennifer changes his life. He withdraws, living with his wife in an old hut. He becomes the father of a boy.

Has he really been lucky? On the one hand he feels himself drawn by love towards his wife and son, on the other hand the past is still strongly alive in him and he feels a longing for that free life. Life in a village or another town is denied him, he would immediately be arrested. But they are worlds apart. She, who comes from a good home and has known high society, is becoming more and more bitter and discontented in the hut. He begins to despair of his life and wonders if it might not be better to send her back to her parents. She is nothing but a hindrance to him. On the other hand he cannot imagine life without her.

These doubts gnaw at him so strongly that he becomes ill with heart disease and shortly afterwards he dies.

He does not doubt for a moment that the wife in his present life is the same one as before. His parents-in-law, too, must be those people he robbed and sent into the wood. In his present life, too, his wife comes from an entirely different background from his. Just as before, he feels under an obligation to her and feels that he has not enough to offer her. Just as before he would really like to send her back to her parents. His parents-in-law treat him with distrust. He blames his wife for his tense relationship with her parents. This makes his wife feel she is unjustly treated. Today, as before, he feels antipathy towards wealthy people, who, in his opinion, exercise power. He has not yet worked at his Karma in a constructive way. His present life is a copy of his former life – although the outer framework and his role in society are today different, the feelings and problems are almost identical.

The consequences of past wrongdoing are serious, whether or not they are followed by legal punishment, because they continue to affect the person in question in his present life or in a later life until he has changed his attitude and his conduct. With Karma, it is not a case of guilt and sins in the ordinary sense, but of recognising that, in everything a person does and thinks, he is affecting himself, even though it is directed towards others.

If anyone thinks it is his right to prey upon others, sooner or later he will come up against people who have the same idea and prey upon him. If anyone thinks that, on account of his position, he has the right to look down on others, and to oppress them, in later lives he will be handed over to people who behave in a similar way towards him. Every arrow we have shot at others will turn into a boomerang, sometimes after such a time that we will have long forgotten our original action. The truth is that all men are of equal value, even though each one is different in his make-up and in the use he makes of his capacities. No one is worth less than another, even if the latter is at a lower level of consciousness. If we wound another person's human dignity, we are at the same time wounding our own.

'What ye have done unto the least of these my brethren, ye have done unto me,' said Christ, and the popular saying goes, 'Do as you would be done by'. What we grant to others will be granted to us, what we are ready to give will be given to us, if we harm others, we ourselves will be harmed. The world around us treats us in exactly the same way as we have treated others. Often you hear people in a difficult situation saying: 'What have I ever done to suffer like this?' Instinctively they sense that their present fate has something to do with past deeds.

Our mistake is in thinking that we can harm other people, because we think that they are worth less, that they have deserved it and that it is only a question of obtaining greater personal advantage from a situation without worrying about them. Another mistake is to believe that if we escape prosecution and punishment in this world, then our deed will have no consequence for us. What we are disregarding is the existence of our conscience. It is our conscience which after death judges our life and which later attracts the confrontation which forces us to pay attention to the consequences of our deeds.

The same laws apply to everyone. These legalities do not happen by chance, they do not come down from Heaven, but they are made by means of 'collective conscience'. We are all equal, that is an incontrovertible truth. We all have the same choice of possible behaviour and experience. Everyone can do as he likes – as far as the laws of the collective unconscious allow. But he must bear the consequences. This means, too, if we have free choice of our fate, that no one forces anything on us or burdens us with anything. We all enjoy freedom of action. From this point of view it is completely senseless to complain about being better or worse endowed mentally and materially, although naturally a lot of people do play this game. No one can raise himself above his present level of consciousness and remain there if his present state of development does not allow it. We have freedom to limit or extend our personal development, but apart from the extent to which we have developed or restricted our possibilities of perception and development, we are all free and self-determined beings. No one can influence us in our actions without our consent. Each one of us is the cause of his own level of consciousness. The inner ceiling is never rigidly fixed. If we allow ourselves to be manipulated or forced into something, this happens only because part of us is in agreement with it.

Often we try to discover the chain of causality for the origins and working out of our fate. We may build atom bombs under the delusion that we are doing something for world peace, or we may see in another person the capacity to bring us enjoyment and happiness and we make ourselves dependent on them, although it should have been our own task. Afterwards we feel we have been let down by life, when things do not turn out as we had falsely imagined they would. However if we will stand aside from onesided thought and action, if we will for once listen to the voice within us and find out which part of us is attracting these misfortunes, then we shall be able to free ourselves from such an unfortunate chain of causality.

There is another side to the picture. One can see oneself and others as always good, positive and friendly and view the world through rose-coloured spectacles. This is also a mistake, because neither life nor man is all good. Good and evil depend on one another, and to act as though there were no other side to the coin means to want to ignore the existence of the cosmos. Applied to Karma, this means that we do not have to pay 'an eye for an eye' for past deeds, but that in the future we may come across the same sort of experiences which we have avoided in the past. If we close our minds to something we shall fall back into a lower level of consciousness. But if we calmly face up to undesirable events and come to terms with them, then we shall rise to a higher level. If we learn to accept unpleasant things as well in our lives, if we learn to recognise suffering for what it is, namely a step on the ladder to ourselves, and strive to deal with every new phenomenon in life, the threat of evil will not actually disappear from the world, but we shall not be helpless in the face of it. On the contrary, we shall make use of the difficulties in order to grow. A person needs the challenge of life in the form of difficulties, crises, struggle, adventure, danger and achievement. If he is not challenged enough, he will develop inward difficulties, illnesses, artificial or imaginary problems and discontent.

So many people make judgments, set moral standards, cannot bear to see others living and loving freely. Suppressed envy may be one of the causes here. What we begrudge to others we carry within ourselves as an unacknowledged wish, whose fulfilment is denied us, since it is always only our own laws which we make. All our thoughts, actions and words determine the environment in which we live, as well as our relationships with other people. Since by reason of some inner harmony we attract certain people and groups, there is also an inner relationship to the group in which we live, so it is not 'fate' that makes us be where we are. We must pause and make up our minds about our present position and our behaviour before we can change anything, for changes can take place only if we are aware of what is not sufficiently developed in us. It may be that we search our little world for the author of our misery and do not recognise ourselves, because the mirror in which we look is clouded. Wherever we may go, we always take ourselves with us. In Zen Buddhism it is said: 'If you cannot find it where you are, where will you go to look for it? There is never any place in the world for anyone, except among one's own kind.' The direction of the journey you must make does not lie in one of the four dimensions. The important thing is to go deeper into the question of what you are and who you are, like turning up the volume on an amplifier.

This also means not simply brushing aside thoughts because they are unpleasant. Whatever we brush aside has also escaped our control. What we do not take any notice of now, we shall one day stumble over. Violent people, for example, are the sort of people who have at some time put far from their minds the idea that they could ever be violent. Looked at in this way, however, one can oneself become the victim of violence; that would only be the other pole of the same thing. Who has never heard it said that culprit and victim attract one another? That is because they live on the same wavelength.

Everything we reject is present, because we have refused to accept that there is such a thing and that it is always around. That is why it is so important for us to become aware of the negative in us and to integrate it, so that it can no longer exercise some magic power of attraction over our lives.

In the same way, everything which we fear is living inside us. We discover that we are bound by anxiety states, whether they be mental, physical or social. Attachment and resistance are two manifestations which spring from the same root. If we offer resistance by not opening our perception, we experience fear, we contract and cramp ourselves and this feeling of being cramped we experience as fear. There is a pull as if from a magnet or from gravity, and this binds us.

For this reason, many people are afraid to open themselves to higher spiritual worlds. They are of the opinion that fear is a signal to avoid something, when really it is a sign that we have avoided it too long. Whether we are aware of it or not, we are one with the cause of everything which exists around us, so it is obviously not by chance that we are born into a certain epoch, with certain tasks and problems facing us. Each one of us was partly responsible for creating wars, persecution and problems with the environment in previous existences and these must now be confronted and tackled constructively by each one of us in later existences. Instead of complaining about unfortunate situations, one should really ask oneself why one should have to come to terms with them in this life, and should try to find out from them the solution to one's personal problem situation.

This would be a significant opportunity to work out one's Karma.

Life is dynamic, not static. In every life we meet with new chances and new challenges, which, if we make significant use of them, will give us the opportunity to develop new powers. Looked at in this way, life is an exciting game – it is only by holding on to old circumstances and convictions or by failing to use possibilities or by not being willing to accept reality, that we make a burden of life so that it then appears static. In too many lives we have left no room for certain vital elements, we have oppressed them and tried to conquer them. These elements later break into our life circumstances with such vehemence that they actually force us to experience the situation and we feel helplessly at their mercy. However Karma may be altered. To use it in order to force ourselves and others into the role of victims or martyrs and to let it rest at that is a colossal misuse. Life is continually offering us new opportunities for further development, if we approach them with good will.

Every thing we have at any time refused will continue to confront us until we have finally integrated it into ourselves. What we have to do in order to become free and sensible is to be willing to accept everything which has entered our consciousness. If we had always done this, then our sub-conscious would never have recorded any painful events and suppressed them from our consciousness and we would not have to deal with the same emotions and suffering again and again. All situations of conflict arise because we have refused to recognise what we ourselves have brought about.

Unfortunately many people, even with the best intentions, attempt to deny what is quite apparent, or to root it out. Many spiritual movements hotly deny the existence of negative intentions and deeds. The real problem is that we are not able to love everything to the same extent, we want to eat the icing off the cake of life and ignore unpleasant experiences. This attitude will always bring with it lack of freedom and a misunderstanding of life; whereas a positive attitude towards life and all its experiences will lead to a real zest for life, since we will realise that at every moment we can mould and direct life afresh.

The Buddhist teachings try to bring people to the view that it is not the world of objects itself which brings evil, but rather the individual's perpetual identification with it. Measured by the goal of painless nirvana, which represents absolute freedom in timeless eternity, all earthly things must naturally be seen as having no effect.

Life too is an intermediate state, that is the state between earthly birth and death. Thus, one life follows another. The whole life process, including thought as a perpetual movement of consciousness, will be seen as being in a continual state of flux. Nothing has real permanence, everything is at every moment in the act of passing away or else it is subject to a new state of becoming.

In Buddhism there are no actual concepts such as good and evil. It is forbidden to Buddhists of all persuasions to kill, to steal or to engage in unnatural sexual intercourse. They are not permitted to lie, to slander, or to speak in an unfriendly or senseless manner. Similarly they must refrain from greed, malice and doubt about the sublimity of 'dharma'. If they are monks or abstemious laymen, they must also avoid taking any strong drink; in China and some other places they do not eat any meat. This idea of Karmic consequences differs from Christian morality in two ways: Firstly, God is not offended by bad deeds, but men must themselves pay the price for their actions. Secondly, there is no question of sin, but only of serious folly, or ignorance. This difference is significant. A Buddhist is not weighed down and terrified by his burden of sins. If he has done wrong he must pay, but the guilt can be fully cancelled out. He is not faced with everlasting damnation and his atonement lies squarely in his own hands.

In practice, this lack of a sense of guilt means that no actions are considered good or bad in themselves but they are seen in a higher connection. Thus, for example, 'unnatural sexual relations' means a practice which will have directly harmful consequences for those who take part or will indirectly harm others.

Buddhist morality revolves round two separate concepts: the duty of compassion and the necessity for self control. Anything which brings harm to others is evil. The special exercises aiming at a correct way of life concern mainly the avoidance of causing harm, which is directed against the individual himself. Causing harm brings on suffering. The person in question aims at the conviction that it is a question of unsuitable behaviour which will harm him and which should no longer be part of his life. An 'evil' snake hidden under the bed still worries the sleeper. It may creep out at any time and start playing its game of seduction.

How does the law of Karma work in practice? To put it simply, you can say that what gives us the most difficulties today is the area in which we formerly did most harm to other people. Since the outside world is only a mirror of the world within us, we meet with unpleasantness and problems only because parts of these lie within us or formerly did so. If friends often leave us in the lurch today, then at one time, we also abandoned our friends. If we lose loved ones through death, then formerly we wished or even brought death on others. If a person keeps on getting into great financial difficulties, that is in return for his having got rich by illegal means or for having squandered a lot of money. If someone is often exploited and deceived in relations with his partners, then he will have treated other partners in this way in the past.

In those areas where a person did something wrong, he will be sensitive and vulnerable. If, when acting as a judge in a previous life, he condemned innocent people, then he will react very strongly if he himself is unjustly accused. It may make him furious or it may depress and worry him. The fact is that it would not worry him personally unless he himself had really accused someone falsely. The cause of vulnerability is (often in psychotherapies) mistakenly sought in the outside world, without taking into account the fact that this very vulnerability demonstrates a weakness in the person's personality. In reality a person suffers only from the consequences of his own action. As we are behaving now or have behaved in the past towards others – what we thought good for them – that we shall sooner or later encounter ourselves.

There are further consequences of earlier wrong behaviour.
Inferiority complex a problem which every psychologist has met. Here an inward feeling is present of having acted wrongly in the past and, as a result of this, the person underrates himself. This inward tendency is picked up by the outside world, which will then also undervalue him and not give him credit for anything. A person with inferiority complex can always go around with the idea that he is not doing his work properly or of failing as a mother or as a father or as a marriage partner. These people are never satisfied with themselves, they are always comparing themselves with other people and have within them a deep-seated feeling of failure.
Difficulties in perception one or more of the sensual organs is blocked. As a result of repression, one's own perception is limited. Shortsighted people often see only what is happening

just round them and have no perception of things further away, which, however, are directly connected with their lives. Long-sighted people perceive everything which is not directly connected with themselves, but things happening just beside them often escape their notice. Longsighted people suppress symptoms of illness and avoid finding out for certain about them. No matter what kind of perception it is, which is limited, it can be extended again by reliving one's own guilt. After a session of reincarnation therapy, many clients notice an alteration in their sight or their hearing.

Suspicion in the form of jealousy, insinuation or doubt, arises only because the person in question reflects in his own repressed behaviour the evil which he imputes to others. Someone who has already betrayed his partner expects betrayal by his present and future partners and suspects that dishonesty and deception will lurk behind everything. One represents one's fear by projecting one's own deeds into one's partner or into other people, because one is unwilling to confess one's own behaviour. To the jealous or suspicious person, he himself is always 'good' and 'just'; insincerity and untrustworthiness would disturb the picture he has of himself. Therefore everything he has done himself, he unconsciously imputes to others. Criticism of others is supposed to reduce his own guilt and deflect attention from it. This background of repression often shows through in one's present life, but in many cases it is solved only by working through previous lives. It can happen that someone in this life always encounters partners who deceive him or leave him in the lurch or that someone suffers from abnormal jealousy without there being any valid reason for it in his present life. The explanation for this emerges when he is regressed to former lives. It then emerges that earlier he, too, betrayed partners and left them in the lurch. Through our present partner we encounter our own previous ego.

Unfounded feelings of guilt: many people have an inexplicably bad conscience, especially when they come into contact with the 'authorities', when they see a policeman or are summoned to appear before a court. They are frightened when they are accused, continually try to justify themselves and are disturbed by the idea that others might talk about them. They behave *de facto* as if they had done something which they have to hide. Before working on guilt in former lives, the therapist first deals with guilt in this life. There are likely to be plenty of things which that person has done and then covered up, such as petty theft, slander, dishonesty, lies and so on. Everything a person has covered up weighs on him, causing a vague feeling of uncertainty and vulnerability. A person will expand visibly if he confesses his negative deeds, adopts better, more ethical points of view and looks for more favourable solutions. People with feelings of guilt have a need for misfortune encountered through other people. They seek out life situations in which something is done to them by others, in order that they themselves may have 'evidence' of how bad they are. Since suppressed guilt leads to uncertainty, repression, lessened perception and further to indifference, foolishness and depression, the recalling of suppressed guilt cancels the self-punishing mechanisms and the person becomes more free, less uncertain and his evaluation of himself and other people becomes more realistic. He no longer needs to feel afraid, especially since the original fear, forming the basis of all others, is the fear of being found out and persecuted for something he has done. Someone with a clear conscience does not know fear. It is the thing to which we do not agree which helps us to define and discover who we are. A person must also take on his own faults and impurity. One cannot live in the endlessness of time without ever having committed a fault. Every fault must be put right, but it will be necessary to go back to its place of origin. It is the suppression of wrongdoing and telling lies about it which later inevitably leads us into difficulties, not the wrongdoing itself. We are the only ones who are responsible for what happens to us. There is absolutely nothing in outward events to determine our feelings and experiences.

To each one of us today the outside world presents the mirror of our former deeds and also the reckoning for them. Thus someone who was formerly a tyrant may today often encounter tyrannical people, who put upon him – this would be the image in the mirror; or else he is despised and injured by those around him – this would be the reckoning. In analysing the problem with regard to previous guilt, both these factors play an equal part. Because man himself is the cause of his own fate, it is only he who can change it by discovering how he brought it about, making himself aware of it and through insight and responsibility examining and giving up his old behaviour. This process of transformation takes place in reincarnation therapy. Previous faults are worked through, thereby removing the necessity for punishment mechanisms, self-limiting factors and compulsory repetitions.

One day forty-year-old Harry came to see me. All his life he had been looking for a meaning to life. He had spent many years with various religious sects and was full of impatience and aggression. On the other hand, he was very much afraid of harming other people. He felt he was too adaptable, that he had lost his original spontaneity and could not achieve what he wanted. He always lived with the idea that he must without fail be liked, he wanted to be thought a 'nice' man but on the other hand he felt himself much too hemmed in in his marriage. He was continually searching for a woman with whom he could form a deep relationship, a relationship such as he had not yet experienced in his present life.

During a reincarnation session, he reported: 'I see myself in Rome, in the amphitheatre, I am wearing a toga. My wealth allows me to live like a lord. I put on great banquets, I am pleasure-seeking and overbearing. There is a crowd of women round me, mainly bought slaves. I treat them like toys and intelligent animals. They are lying at my feet and I am fondling them without really being sincere with them.

The scene changes. I am a politician, I see myself making speeches. I am a senator with special functions. I am married to a woman who is just my ideal. She has long black hair worn in plaits. I am delighted with her, but she does not want anything more to do with me. In particular she does not agree with me arranging all these banquets. I have to keep defending myself and explaining to her that this is part of the life of a senator. If I did not arrange these feasts, then I am afraid I would not be sufficiently well-known and accepted. She reproaches me with my affairs and I try to explain to her that these are unimportant, that it would not upset our relationship; but my wife says that they certainly would upset it.

For these reasons she is now leaving me. I had not been expecting that at all. It makes me sad and pains me that she does not want to have anything more to do with me. Besides, it wounds my pride, I am afraid of 'losing face'. My wife was a person of so-called high-standing, completely independent of me and for this reason I am not able to get her back.

After this I feel weakness, I long for her and feel that life has no sense in it.'

After this session of recalling the past, he said: 'That is the woman I am inwardly looking for. It touched me deeply to have lost her through my own indifference. Of course I was making excuses when I said that it was essential for me to give those banquets. I regretted it afterwards and felt aggression in me, which I directed above all against myself. In my present life it is just the same. I become aggressive if something does not go according to my wishes. I am very intolerant of myself and will not allow myself anything. Even today I often make excuses, I do not stand by myself. Today it is completely impossible for me to establish an intensive relationship with a woman. I still have the feeling of being 'better' than other people, which makes them in their turn aggressive against me and they boycott me.

Here is another case in which we can observe the working out of Karma:

One day a forty-year old man came to see me; he had just been divorced. When he was young he had broken off his education because he 'hated' school. As a child he had had infantile paralysis. He was impatient with other people and became easily excited. He had broken off contact with his father very early because he remembered him as being very authoritarian. In one of our reincarnation sessions he relived the following experiences: 'I see foreign children, black children, boys. I am treating them like cattle. I am whipping and beating them. I am a slave dealer. I can see myself getting drunk, while the black children are being driven on to the ship. I am the captain of this ship. There are about a hundred children disappearing into the hold. Someone or other is taking care of the weak ones, they are being killed before we sail. The slaves are taken to Holland.

On the return voyage I take weapons on board. I'll do absolutely anything to earn money. I would have taken white people too and sold them, if that had been possible. I am always on the go, because everything to do with my relatives gets on my nerves. I don't like going home, my wife shudders at the sight of me. When I am at home I do nothing but drink, I go around bawling and tyrannising my family. At some time or other I took my son with me on the ship, he was a weakling, a little chap. I handed him over to the crew to make a man of him. I did not worry about him any more and then later he was killed in an accident. My relatives reproached me for it, but I would not put up with that. I simply made off. Life went on like that until one day, when I was drunk, I fell off the deck. I hurt my leg, it felt as though red-hot rods were boring into it (infantile paralysis in real life). My leg was stuck between the edge of the ship and the harbour wall. I never got well again.'

What this man did to the slaves and to other people, too, especially his son, in that incarnation is done by analogy to him, in real life, by his father. His father was a hard man and never did anything but make demands. My client also met with the authoritarian type among his colleagues at work and he continually had to stand up for himself and make his way against opposition. Discontent and restlessness gave him no peace in this life.

In many psychological conversations former lives come up without necessarily being recognised as such. The comparisons which patients use to describe their situations and difficulties in life are often taken unconsciously from experiences in former lives:

'It is as though someone had stuck a spear into my heart.'
'I feel I have been betrayed and sold.'
'That will be the death of me.'
'That is a catastrophe.'
'I shall die if he leaves me.'
'It is as though he were looking down from his platform and judging me.'
'I am afraid all the time of being deceived.'
'There is a wall all round me.'
'That's unbearable.'
'I feel I have been trapped.'
'I can't manage it.'
'You can't trust anyone.'
'It is dangerous to tell the truth.'
'I am being pulled from all sides.'
'I am afraid my husband is not going to come back any more.'
'I am afraid she is going to leave me.'
'I feel I have been cast out without any right to exist.'
'My head feels as if it were stuck between two planks.'
'Nobody likes me.'

These are just a few examples of things people say which point to previous lives. These clear and vivid descriptions often come straight from earlier experiences. Such fears and feelings cannot be explained by logic and by the intellect. In this life, the patient has not experienced anything which would provide a foundation for these fears.

In reincarnation therapy, we proceed on the assumption that there is justification for every fear and every problem which a person has; that there is a concrete situation in which this fear

was understandable and applicable. However, since the subconscious mixes up time and place and cannot distinguish
between the past and the present, it reflects the fear or the
reaction to a life situation long past as soon as similar elements
appear in the present situation. Inexplicable fears and emotions
are often resolved very quickly in reincarnation therapy.

Former lives come to light in situations which are repeated,
such as fears, problems and conflicts, and also in dreams and in
much wishful thinking. Preferences and aversions are similarly
the expression of previous experiences.

Self-repeating dreams are impressions from previous lives in
which unresolved material is recycled over and over again. A
client kept on seeing herself in a dream dressed in a vest and
thought this very unpleasant. The dream was explained when
we worked through an event in a previous life in which she
represented someone in authority who was suddenly deprived
of power and was unable to cope with this. She described her
feelings after being deprived of power in these words: 'I'm
standing here as if I were in my vest.' This feeling, together
with the pictured image, was recorded in the subconscious and
expressed in the present dreams.

Wishful thinking and illusions may be genuine former identities
or experiences or they may just be dream ones, which the
consciousness fixes on after too many negative and traumatic
experiences. If someone today has a compulsion to be rich and
famous, he may really have been rich and famous in a previous
life. But it is essential when regressing to tackle the underlying
problem, namely poverty and lack of importance, since fixation
on the positive is in reality suppression of the negative.

*Predelictions for places, countries, languages, styles in art, periods
in history or else aversions to these:* generally one can assume
that, in the case of a predeliction for a country, or a period, one
is more likely to have experienced something positive there in a
previous life and that in the case of an aversion one is more
likely to have gathered negative experiences, although this is
not always the case. One may also have a longing for a certain
country or landscape, because one had a loss there, which one
was unable to cope with or because one was unable to complete
a task. One unconsciously longs to be back in order to end this
experience. Looking at it from the viewpoint of polarity, too,
our preferences tell us a lot about our dislikes and about our
actual problems.

Distinguishing features It is interesting to observe how a person's physique and features sometimes resemble those of a race to which he does not belong or have any hereditary trace of in this life. Among western people there are types with almond eyes, high cheekbones and black hair, who could pass themselves off without difficulty as from the Far East or Egypt. There are people who feel completely at home with the gypsies and themselves display similar traits, both of appearance and of character, others who look like South Sea Islanders and – how could it be otherwise – spend their holidays in the South Seas. An interesting point is the relationship between the 'other' people and these people who bear their outward traits – the natives of the country in question accept these people and treat them like one of themselves. Language barriers are easily overcome.

Talents Talents of every kind point to former experiences in that particular field. An Albert Einstein can scarcely have spent only one life dealing with physics and mathematics and it is just as unlikely that Wolfgang Amadeus Mozart would have been able to obtain so much musical knowledge at one stroke during the first years of his life as to enable him to give his first concert at the age of five, unless he had brought with him previous knowledge in that field from a former life. Anything which comes to us easily is something which is already familiar to us from somewhere else. Basically we do not learn any more but just remember what we have known before. Even inventions are often memories from the past. The idea of how a thing might function is related to what one has already seen at some time. In this connection, it should be noted that in former times, as well as today, there were civilisations which were both technically and spiritually greatly superior to our own and that there are, therefore, the most varied stages of development.

Aversions and blocks in certain fields of knowledge may also have completely negative roots in previous lives. If an astronomer in the Middle Ages was executed for having theories too advanced for the time, he may in his present life have a definite block where astronomy or mathematics is concerned. His knowledge brought him death in the past, so his subconscious concludes that it is better to have nothing whatever to do with these fields. Or someone who was previously a victim of technology will have no appreciation for technology today. He may also not be able to deal with technical equipment and appliances, he may be afraid of them or he may harm them by mistake. His attitude to technology suffers badly.

Similar phenomena may occur if a person has harmed others with the help of technology in a previous life; if, for example, he has oppressed or destroyed them.

All our crucial interests as well as our blocks are probably based on our previous history.

Children often give informative accounts of their previous lives, since they are still in close contact with their past and have not yet been brought up in any particular faith. There are some children who have the impression, quite early on, that their parents are not their real parents and who do not feel that they belong in the parental home. They are unconsciously still clinging to another life and have not yet settled down here. Children may early on display tyrannical tendencies and want to order their parents about. They are persisting in a previous domineering role and believe they still have the right to rule others.

Children, also, often have pronounced fears and depressions, which do not fit in with their present lives. Past experiences, which aroused fear, are still quite fresh in their memory. It is amazing how many children are afraid of war, although no war was threatening when they were in the womb. This may be expressed in the form of a child's dreams, which may contain soldiers in quite specific uniforms and caps. Children dream about being persecuted, about being murdered, about religious gatherings and political actions. Of course children can pick things up from the television, but their subconscious would not react so strongly to them if corresponding things had not already been stored up.

If you ask a child: 'If you had lived before, how do you imagine your life would have been?', you will get astonishingly detailed accounts including concrete problems. In my experience, children are never really opposed to the idea of having lived before; but over the years the conscious, rational part of their personality becomes more strongly marked and they lose direct access to their subconscious.

5.

Reincarnation and Psychotherapy

If we try in the following pages to compare reincarnation therapy with psychotherapy, we shall not be able to establish any general comparison, because psychotherapy exhibits a variety of forms and a variety of possibilities of therapy. For this reason we will deal in a comparative way only with behavioural therapy in order to see what differences there are.

To quote from the book *Everything Was all Right – So What Went Wrong?* by Fanita English: 'A few years ago a young man went into a shop in Texas, bought a gun, climbed up a tower and began to shoot at the passers-by.

'In the course of the ensuing police evidence it emerged that this nice young man had not only shot eleven people, who happened to be passing by, but before that he had killed his own mother and wife.

'He left behind a statement in which with touching helplessness he expressed his deep longing for consolation and love. In it he complained that his mother and his wife had neglected him after having previously 'loved' him. It turned out that on the previous day he had tried to get help from a psychiatrist, but had been sent away as simply a "depressive case" – which indeed he was, someone going round and round in a circle. The psychiatrist had not recognised that he was just about to behave in a manner which was exactly the opposite of his own type. Because of an excessive hunger for attention, he had finally given in to his basic, unrecognised madness. When the police overpowered him and took him away, he appeared quite gentle and kind again. He had gone back to his childhood ego and expected the parent ego, ie the police, to give him attention and protection, even if this should happen in a negative way.'

Behaviour therapy seizes on a person's actual behaviour at any given moment and classifies it as suitable or unsuitable. In this way the important role of influencing and opinion-forming is assigned to the environment. This does not take into account the fact that this person can choose to react against environmental influences and thereby reduce them and also that he has within him, and is able to develop, inclinations which are contrary to the wishes of the environment. Behavioural therapy proceeds on the assumption that a person, who thinks that his environment has failed him, is suffering from a loss of satisfaction, to which he is reacting with 'conflict'. Here his growing frustration is often seen as the result of his own inability to find reliable partners. It is assumed that such a person is inwardly leaping from one ego-state to another. Everyone concerned is then astonished at his outburst of passion and cannot imagine that such a thing could happen. According to the behaviourist psychologists, fight/flight behaviour is biologically rooted and can be reckoned with as a behavioural possibility. They see it arising as a reaction to fear, loss or anxiety. Since most people bear within them fear, and anxiety and especially fear of loss, these people would accordingly all be potential murderers.

According to Jungian depth psychology, the picture is rather different. The case would be judged in something like the following way: since it is a question of someone who is usually calm and rational, one concludes that this person was educated in such a way as to make him an acceptable human being, that is a human being who should always be 'nice and docile'. But since there is 'good' and 'bad' stored up in everyone, the 'bad' can be suppressed only to a certain extent and in times of 'inner distress' it will break out violently. This means that as a result of being violently swamped by evil, a person is incapable of sound judgement at the time when the deed is committed.

As I have already tried to establish by citing other cases, reincarnation therapy takes quite a different viewpoint. It is based on the assumption that this young man and the people connected with him have already known each other in a previous life. In that previous life there were unresolved emotions and deeds of violence, which are now being continued or countered in this way. A shock when his life was in danger or an unsuccessful action may today appear as a life-saver, because it can give the illusion of being the 'stronger'. It may have been a former experience from a 'time of war' which broke through and caused this behaviour in the young man.

Many people find psychotherapy weird. A process, in the course of which a patient is released from despair and given realistic hope, seems like magic, beyond the scope of reason, and there are many people who would prefer to believe that such a thing is simply not possible. But most of these methods of treatment are based on solid, straightforward principles and reincarnation therapy is here no exception. It is a therapeutic method in no way related to the occult, even though, like the latter, it accepts the possibility of being born again.

Like many other forms of psychotherapy, reincarnation therapy presupposes the existence of the subconscious. Often we cannot remember trigger events which call traumas to life. Only the 'scars' are to be seen – in the form of behavioural disturbances. But the events have not been forgotten. They have only been suppressed and are sunk in the subconscious. To my mind, the most interesting aspect of reincarnation therapy is that it forms a connection between mind and body. Most doctors accept the fact that the mind has a profound influence on the body – stomach ulcers and migraine are well-known examples of psychosomatic illnesses.

Reincarnation therapy confirms this, but it also demonstrates the opposite possibility, namely that a physical injury in a former life may be at the root of a present psychological problem. Body and mind are so intimately connected that it is necessary to investigate the reciprocal action they have had on one another in the past.

People who, from unconscious motives, are forced to suppress many things, use up an enormous amount of energy in the process. The fact that confrontation with what is being suppressed has been removed from one's consciousness leads to irrational belligerence, to the rejection and combatting of the realities of life, of facts and standards, which would really require an objective elucidation carried out in full consciousness.

Those who suppress things do not first seek the solution to their problems in their own personality, but rather they require a scapegoat to be made responsible for all the things which are not right in the world. However, this is the beginning of a disastrous mechanism. The weaker an individual is, the less he can cope with the truths and realities of life and the more he will suppress. The more we, as individuals, suppress, the more we shall be hemmed in; we shall lose opportunities for development and become aggressive. Frustration due to lack of ego-strength and emotional blocks resulting from suppression and impeded development of one's life, frequently lead to depression, often hiding behind aggressive behaviour and destructive attitudes. Even if no depressive mood is apparent, a disturbed relationship will develop towards certain sections of the environment. In order to free ourselves from the pressure of emtoional blocks, we turn to projection, which helps us to find the scapegoat, or at least we find someone at whose door we can lay the blame. It is always the others who are the bad ones, which is why we reject them, laugh at them, mock them, shut them out, make them seem ridiculous or else we find even worse ways of 'paying out' the wicked world around us. Reincarnation therapy is often accused of shifting the scapegoat into a previous life and, therefore, unable to be particularly helpful; but this is not true. Let us for a moment place reincarnation therapy alongside the other popular psychotherapies, in order to demonstrate that reincarnation therapy stands up very well in comparison with other forms of psychotherapy.

Just in the last few years the number of different forms of therapy has grown and it looks as though we are not yet at the end of this expansion. More and more new forms are appearing publicly and the layman has difficulty in recognising that these new therapies are little more than variations on old forms. Unfortunately there is no unified line in psychotherapy. The different kinds of treatment range from treatment of the symptoms of illness and the many and varied self experimental groups right up to self realisation. Psychotherapy today is whatever a psychotherapist practises.

The oldest forms of psychotherapy popular today derive from Sigmund Freud and his pupils, Alfred Adler and Karl Gustav Jung; they go under the title of classic, deep-psychological methods. With them were associated additional methods, behavioural and humanistic therapies, group and family therapies and some others. The most widespread ones are:

1.0 Insight therapies based on deep psychology

1.1 Psychoanalysis according to Sigmund Freud

1.2 Psychoanalysis as analysis of the ego according to Karen Horney (Erich Fromm, Sullivan)

1.2.1 Psychoanalysis as analysis of the ego according to Anna Freud, Erick Erikson, D. Rapaport

1.3 Psychology of the individual according to Adler

1.4 Analytical psychology according to C.G. Jung

1.5 Catathymic picture life according to Leuner

2.0 Humanistic additions
2.1 Gestalt therapy according to Perls
2.2 Conversational therapy according to Rogers
2.3 Transpersonal psychology
2.4 Psycho-drama according to Moreno
2.5 Transaction analysis according to Eric Berne
2.6 Bioenergetics according to Loroen
3.0 Behavioural therapy
3.1 Behavioural therapy based on the theory of learning
3.2 Cognitive behavioural therapy
3.3 Rationally emotive therapy (RET) according to Ellis

Depth psychology and the humanistic therapies are called insight therapies, because they are based on the assumption that a person's behaviour is disturbed only because he is not aware of the motives for his actions and thoughts. Psychoanalysis stresses above all factors lying in childhood, whereas the humanistic therapies lay emphasis on present behavioural problems. An important role is played by personal meeting with the 'Thou', inter-personal contact and a person's relations with the world. For this reason you will find with the humanists much group work and body awareness training, role-playing, etc. which should facilitate discovering and developing the self.

Behavioural therapy is based on the psychology of learning and on experimental psychology in general. For this reason it is also described as a scientific method. It is based on the premise that all behaviour is acquired and it does not concern itself with biographical factors. Whilst at first behaviour alone was observed and modified, later on cognitive and emotional factors were also admitted.

1.1 Freudian Psychoanalysis Freudian psychoanalysis is based on the personality of Freud and the spirit of the age at the turn of the century. It is materially oriented. Its basic assumptions are: libido (energy of the sexual instincts), later also the death instinct, the genetic developmental urges (oral, anal, phallic, genital phase) and the teaching of emotional disturbance and neuroses, which influenced the whole of psychiatry, depth and developmental psychology and educational theory. The best-known is the so-called Oedipus complex. Many of Freud's assumptions do not stand up against later scientific discoveries, research and the psychologically orientated experiences of astrology and reincarnation.

Freud makes a distinction between the unconscious, the pre-conscious and the conscious as also between the id, the ego and the super-ego. According to him emotional energy, which corresponds to the id, increases, decreases, becomes displaced and is capable of being eliminated. It insists absolutely on immediate satisfaction. The libido, the energy of the sexual instincts, goes through certain phases during a child's development. Unresolved conflicts in these phases are the cause of neuroses. During his lifetime Freud shifted emphasis from the libido to the ego as the centre of inward psychic conflict. The ego, as central decision-making authority of conscious action in the form of self-control must mediate between the urgent desires of the id and the normalising (morally and ethically based) restrictions of the SUPER-EGO.

As techniques, Freud and his pupils used free association and dream analysis. Other important components are transference and counter-transference and the analysis of resistance.

The patient lies on the couch, the analyst sits behind him. The patient has to say everything that comes into his mind without censoring it at all (= free association). The therapist has to connect to the patient's weakened ego, so that suppressed childhood experiences come to the surface and the adult ego, adapting to reality, overcomes the infantile fear of expressing the libido.

The patient develops when he is made aware of his unconscious resistances and comes to terms with them, whilst the emotional experiences are transferred to the analyst. Counter-transference consists in the sensitive reaction of the analyst to what the client has transferred to him.

It is the analyst's task to guide the patient in such a way that his emotional stress is no longer suppressed, but can be controlled. In this connection the therapist should always be neutral and objective, i.e. he should refrain from criticism based on value-judgment, but this does not rule out confronting the patient with his own behaviour.

This passive, reserved attitude on the part of the therapist means that the psychoanalysis will last from two to five years with three to five sessions a week.

1.2 Ego Analysis Ego analysis is a further development of

psychoanalysis by Karen Horney, Erich Fromm, Sullivan and W. Silverberg. It is practised chiefly in the USA and is also called neopsychoanalysis.

This no longer assigns a primary role to sex. It emphasises more strongly the need and the capability of the patient to exercise control over his environment and the satisfaction of his desires. It also concerns itself more strongly with the patient's conditions of life, whereas these were neglected in classical psychoanalysis.

For example, Karen Horney says that women do not envy men on account of their penises, but because of their greater professional, social and cultural possibilities. The neopsychoanalysts question the assumption that it is urges alone which drive the life of the soul and they assume that human behaviour is the result also of feelings, aims and values. They question the supremacy of the id over the ego and ascribe a certain autonomy to the ego. They also say that Freud exaggerated the importance of childhood experiences. Karen Horney sees in neurosis a current problem which a patient can be prevented from addressing if one enquires too deeply into his childhood. In her view, people do not inevitably become neurotic from yielding to their urges, but they may, if they fail to adapt to their present socio-cultural milieu or do not come to terms with the fears and tensions connected with it. She distinguishes between three courses which the neurosis may take: self-abnegating, expansive or resigned. Therapy should help a person to uncover such neurotic resolutions and to recognise who he really is. This is a first step towards self-realisation.

1.2.2.   Anna Freud was chiefly concerned with child analysis and the defensive mechanisms of the ego. She saw the super-ego as the originator of neuroses. It is the task of the therapist to weaken or moderate the super-ego.

1.3 *Psychology of the individual according to Adler*   Adler brought social aspects into psychoanalysis. He too saw the origins of neuroses in childhood; not in sex however, but in socio-economic disadvantage which manifested, among other things, in feelings of inferiority, helplessness and neurosis as a defence against the demands of the environment. Through social recognition and striving for respect and power, the patient tries to compensate for inferiority complexes. Through therapy, which includes strongly educational aspects and pays attention to posture, gestures, mimicry, etc, the patient has to learn to take up a positive position in the community. Adler did not enquire into the causes but into the goal: 'What purpose does it serve?'

1.4 Analytical Psychology   C.G. Jung began the holistic view of man, which was continued in humanistic and transpersonal psychology and particularly in reincarnation therapy.

Like psychoanalysis, analytical therapy makes use of dream interpretation and free association. Beside the personal unconscious, Jung envisaged a collective unconscious, containing latent, inherited, memories of past human development, manifesting in symbols and myths, the so-called archetypes.

The aim of this therapy is to make conscious and integrate the suppressed, inferior, dark and undeveloped aspects of personality, ie reconciliation with the 'shadow' and the abolition of projection. It strives for the development of the whole personality = individuation, within the boundaries a person has to observe, and the awakening of the creative potential from the collective unconscious.

2.1 Gestalt Therapy   Here, as with other humanistic therapies, the creative aspects of a person are stressed. Psychic problems arise from frustrations and the denial of emotional needs. Perls starts with the assumption that we all bring our needs and desires with us into every situation. Our feelings have an effect on everything which happens. The here and now is at the central point, man is responsible for his own behaviour.

By the use of various techniques, the therapist makes his client aware of his own evasive behaviour; fear of social relations should be reduced; personal, emotional needs should be experienced and satisfied. The person should find his way to wholeness again and lead a fulfilled life.

2.2 Conversation Therapy   Conversation therapy is also called client-based therapy. The client sits directly opposite the therapist, so that eye-contact may be established. It assumes that learning processes which have had an unfavourable outcome have led to behavioural disturbances. In a warmly sympathetic atmosphere of positive esteem, the client should become aware of his conflicts, while expressing his deep emotions, which the therapist reflects back to him. In this way the emotional conflicts, which hinder the client in his process of self-realisation should be removed step by step. The client should use his own strength to bring about an alteration in himself so that his ideal picture of himself and the person he actually is, are integrated.

2.3 Transpersonal Psychology Transpersonal therapy, which arises from existential analysis and from the psychosynthesis of R. Assagioli, embraces everything known today under the title 'New Age'. To it belongs also Dürckheim's 'initiatory therapy'.

Their techniques consist of group games, body awareness training, meditation, biofeedback, artistic expression including religious and spiritual experiences. Extrasensory perceptions and various states of consciousness (through meditation, yoga, trance, drugs) are included. They proceed on the assumption that a person basically has the possibility of realising his innate capabilities. If this is impeded, it leads to crises in his life and behavioural disturbances. Transpersonal psychology goes beyond the personal and concerns itself with extra-personal = transcendental experiences and dimensions of consciousness. Everything should be accepted, intensively experienced and then relinquished; opposites should be resolved on a higher plane = synthesis. Through dispensing with barriers and looking at the whole and experiencing it, a person should become calmer, should rest in himself and dissolve into the All One.

2.4 Psychodrama From his work with children and their spontaneous and creative play, Moreno developed the method called psychodrama. This theatrical method and its emphasis on the client experiencing the 'here and now' influenced all other humanistic therapies.

Acting out and experiencing problems and conflicts on a pretended stage should produce a healing effect, freeing the person from experiences which are weighing down on him. Psychodrama consists of three phases: 1. Initial phase: warm up, finding the problem. 2. Action phase: action, play, treatment of the problem. 3. Subsequent counselling phase: discussion and integration.

2.5 Transaction Analysis Transaction analysis originated with Berne. Three states of experience and behaviour are postulated: the child-ego, the parent-ego, the adult ego.

The communication of this ego in speech and in play (singly or in groups) is analysed (script analysis) as transaction patterns (play) and life designs (messages, decisions). Recognition of this communication pattern should bring about a change in behaviour.

2.6 Bioenergetics Bioenergetics is a further development by Pierrakos and Lowen of the orgone (vegeto-) therapy of W. Reich. All stress, whether psychic or physical, causes tensions in the body. In the case of continual stress, eg through unresolved emotional conflicts and continual frustrations, these tensions do not resolve themselves but manifest physically as muscle strains. The basic pattern for this behaviour is thought to arise in early childhood, especially from unsatisfied needs. By means of physical exercises, breathing and shouting, which are worked through by psychoanalysis, the client should be able to 'enjoy life with zest'.

3.1 Behavioural Therapy With the aid of behavioural therapy, the client should be able to alter unsuitable modes of behaviour, attitudes and feelings, which manifest openly in concrete life situations. Behavioural therapy considers it harmful to stir up the repressed past. The treatment is preceded by an extensive behavioural analysis and a plan of therapy. Various techniques are employed according to each particular problem. The best known and most successful are: 1. Systematic desensitising in the case of fears and phobias; 2. Training in self-assurance (assertion) in the case of unself-assured behaviour; 3. Aversion conditioning in the case of addictions (smoking, alcohol, etc) overeating and bad habits; 4. Operative conditioning – the reinforcing of desired reactions and the diminuation of undesirable ones in the case of observable behaviour by means of reward and punishment – in the case of children and hospital patients; 5. Model learning = learning new reactions and unlearning old ones by observing and copying models; for obtaining social skills in the case of fears and phobias; in the education of children.

3.2 Cognitive Behavioural Therapy Since behaviour cannot be explained by assumptions solely based on educational theory, behavioural therapists began to integrate cognitive elements into their methods. Here it is a case of an alteration in the internal patterns of valuation, assimilating and argumentation which lie at the basis of this behaviour. From this arose the behavioural therapy methods of model learning and training in self-confidence.

3.3 Rational-emotive Therapy Ellis had 'very little' success with psychoanalysis and turned to neopsychoanalytic and behavioural therapeutic methods. From his criticism of psychoanalysis and the reflection of his personal experience with patients, he developed rational emotive therapy as a strongly directive form of therapy, based on rational dispute with emotive, behaviouristic elements.

A central factor of the genesis and maintenance of psychic disturbances is thinking in the form of irrational attitudes and appraisals (eg polarised thought, exaggerations, over-generalisations, taking everything personally). This can become the cause of tensions, since such people are convinced and see all events in the light of such assumptions, as for example 'There's no sense in any of it', 'What a worthless person I am'.

In therapy these irrational ideas and their destructive effect should be uncovered. With Ellis it is a matter of basic, cognitive restructuring. For this he makes use of imagination exercises, confrontation, refutation, counter-indoctrination and re-education.

What does reincarnation therapy have in common with other therapies?

Primarily, reincarnation therapy shares with psychoanalysis and analytical psychology the technique of free association. However, with RT there is no transference and counter-transference with resulting transference neurosis by way of the therapist, but rather the client has direct recognition of the origin of his troubles.

In M. Netherton's technique, which has similarity with Ellis's procedure, ie it is carried out in a well-aimed and strongly directive way, RT is economical and saves time. It needs only about a tenth of the time taken by psychoanalysis in order to solve the problems.

Freud's so-called 'Oedipus complex' (together with many of the assumptions of psychoanalysis) presents itself in quite a different light because it is conditioned by connections with previous lives. Unlike psychoanalysis, RT does not connect symptoms of illness with early childhood, but goes back to their origin in previous lives and possible reactivation in pregnancy.

As with the humanistic therapies and rational-emotive therapy, RT takes present problems as its starting-point, but it goes a step further into previous life. Netherton, like rational emotive therapy, plays great attention to irrational attitudes and guiding principles, as for example, 'It is all senseless', or 'I shall never manage that.' Like analytic and transpersonal psychology, RT tries to understand and heal the whole person and not just certain symptoms. However, it achieves this only by regressions in a state of relaxation and by emotionally and cognitively working through the problem in a dialogue between the client and the therapist. If a client wants to have just a certain symptom treated, then, as in behavioural therapy, the therapist will do just that. As in the humanistic therapies and rational-emotive therapy, RT emphasises the responsibility of the client for his own problems and deeds.

A responsible and well-trained RT therapist will carry out the therapy in a climate of warm sympathy and openness. Like behavioural therapy, RT takes as its starting-point that all behaviour is acquired and can be modified; only it does it by regression and by making a person aware of the occurrence which laid the foundation of his unsuitable conduct. As with behavioural therapy and rational emotive therapy, the client should imagine a succession of fear-dispelling stimuli. Instead of exposing the client to the real situation as in systematic desensitising and confronting him with increasingly difficult situations, the occurrence (or occurrences) connected with such fear-inspiring experiences is sought out in a previous life and worked through, possibly through several lives, until the original occurrence which caused the symptoms has been found. As in behavioural therapy and rational emotive therapy, the client is now and then given 'homework' to do, eg in the case of phobias, to expose himself gradually to the actual fear-inspiring situation or, in the case of unpleasant habits and addictions, to keep a so-called control chart.

Altogether one could say that RT embraces the essential features of all the therapies which have proved their worth in practice, provided they are carried out in a responsible manner.

In every therapy, we are faced with the question: how can there be any genuine improvement unless the original problem is recognised and the real troubles are eliminated with it?

The second dilemma is that of the therapist judging and condemning. He adopts an attitude towards the client's problems, diagnoses them, gives a commentary on them and may in some circumstances actually succumb to the problem, if he inadvertently projects his own problems on the client. However every judgment erects barriers.

In reincarnation therapy, we try to consider all forms of expression of the unconscious. It is a question of opening up channels in order to penetrate into regions containing long-forgotten traumas, experiences of shock and one's own guilt. During reincarnation therapy, ideas and thoughts flow into the consciousness. Nothing extraneous enters; what is revealed is what has been personally experienced. While the clients are speaking and reporting former experiences, they are conscious of what they are saying, even though the detailed description may not match the emotional intensity of the experience.

This way of opening up channels produces an even more alert consciousness, since the information, which up to now has been unconscious, is re-experienced and expressed. The person's horizon, his higher self, broadens as he gets to know more and more parts of himself. Experiences in RT give us three guiding principles: 1. Do not make any comparisons. 2. Do not make any judgments. 3. Free yourself from the necessity to arrange everything in a rational, analytic way.

Over and over again during our upbringing we are forced to enter into competition with other people: at school, in further education, the housewife who would like to keep her house even more perfectly, the young man who wants a more powerful 'machine' than his friends. Everywhere we compare ourselves with others; we want to be faster, better, stronger, more agile, healthier, wealthier and a lot more besides. But every comparison deflects us from our own humanity and the development of our own personality. It drives us into merciless competition and we do not realise that we are really letting life slip by. Every society has its own criteria, according to which people measure themselves. If, physically or mentally, we do not measure up to the norm, we suffer from inferiority. And yet it is we ourselves who produce this inferiority, because it is not the supposed rejection on the part of other people which causes us the real pain, but the fact that we do not accept ourselves.

Failure to accept the situation as it is or else to accept one's own nature lies at the root of every human problem. It is only by accepting the situation as it is that one can then alter it. For this reason, we must learn to accept ourselves as we are and not to compare ourselves with the world around us. Even less should we put ourselves under pressure by setting ourselves unrealistic standards and expectations. This will only lead to further dissatisfaction with ourselves.

Every person brings with him, from his past, judgments of himself and his actions by the world around him, some of which were painful and led to condemnation by higher authorities. On account of these painful experiences, there builds up in a person an inner resistance to being judged from outside and this finds expression in an unpleasant feeling. If the mind's reality does not equate with physical reality, confrontation with the worldly reality must result. As soon as the mind refuses to accept an actual event, it cuts itself off from it, its vision is distorted and no longer accords with the truth. This leads to the experience of not being understood, to isolation and pain. Pain is the inability to accept a real event, the inability to live in harmony with what actually is. Such a mind does not have enough tolerance and kindness to concede to another level of reality its right to exist. As soon as pain is discernable, the person feels bound to resort to strong, defensive mechanisms. Suppression and vindication increase his difficulties and lead to obduracy and depression. The ability to experience 'it is' and to allow oneself to be carried along by it, is a sign of the beginning of unity between soul, body and mind. It is the first initiation into a natural state of being.

Through an inner mechanism of vindication, a person will often cling to the most senseless points of view and keep on using these against all reason, even when life has long ago proved that they are useless. However, on the way to self recognition one must become aware of wrong ways of seeing things and must give these up. If the therapist wants to help his client to examine the rightness and validity of old perceptions, he can do this only if his attitude is free from prejudice and bias. For this reason, the second guiding principle: 'Do not make judgments' is equally valid for the therapist and the client. The client must be given the opportunity of questioning the judgments he made in this life and in previous lives, of evaluating them afresh and of replacing them by new, less restrictive modes of viewing.

Our reactions to good and evil, to the beautiful and the ugly, to right and wrong are answers we have learnt, which have something to do with the unfolding of our personality, with the level of consciousness of our soul.

Too rigid judgments are an attempt by the soul to repel unpleasant realities. These judgments become insuperable walls, which isolate the person from the outside world. They are the expression of a fear of reality; but fear leads to loss of freedom. For this reason, rigid judgments and spiritual freedom cannot be reconciled. A firm spirit can grant being to all things and does not make generalised judgments. On the contrary it spontaneously assesses every solution by intuition. RT is a good medium for tracing antiquated opinions and modes of conduct.

A further obstacle in life is the need to rationalise and put everything in order. This third guiding principle does not demand that one should diminish or limit one's capacity for insight and understanding. It does, however, warn against continually feeling the need to arrange and hold on to things originating in some time before this life. Absolute knowledge and understanding are, of course, qualities of the soul. The desire to put things in order interposes itself between the observer and whatever presents itself to his consciousness, and blocks the way. It is a sign of a need to keep in control, rather than to allow oneself to be carried along by the reality of higher consciousness. If we free ourselves from the necessity of keeping in control, in the same way that we free ourselves from making comparisons and judgments, we can experience what reality is – and how many new realities there can be, if only we allow them. We often make reason responsible for our need to remain in control. But reason itself is not the cause of our need to rationalise. Rather it is our inability to agree without reservation to things as they are. Too strongly marked reason is an attempt to block out painful reality; one clings to rationality after emotion has been overcome by reality. For this reason, strongly marked reason is no cause of hindrance, but rather a challenge to choose a therapy, which pays more attention to the neglected parts of one's own personality.

Let us now take a look at the system of judging and condemning by means of an example drawn from my practice. The client gives as her main worry, problems about food and weight.

(T: therapist; P: patient)

T. We will now make connection with the experience which is the cause of your present difficulties. At some time during the nine months of pregnancy, your mother had thoughts and feelings which you picked up. We will now direct your subconscious to make connection with this point in time. You are already there. You are already conscious of your mother's thoughts about food and excessive weight. Tell me the first words which come into your head.

P. Oh! Oh! She is in pain.

T. Leave her to it, let her cry. Tell me the words your mother is saying.

P. I don't like her body. She is so fat. I hate her body.

T. Who is thinking or saying that?

P. My mother.

T. What is she thinking or saying?

P. I am so fat. I hate my body.

T. What are the next words?

P. No, no, not that.

T. Tell me the next words which come into your head.

P. Mummy, help me.

T. What is your mother feeling now?

P. She is feeling better.

T. We will go back. Tell me the first part of the body which occurs to you. Where your mother feels pain.

P. Her belly. It is hard.

T. If your mother were to speak aloud while she was crying, what words would she say?

P. Help me. (The next words) No, no, I don't want that. (The next words) I don't want to die. Why did he do that?

T. What does your mother mean by 'why did he do that?'

P. She means my father. He has made her pregnant. (The next words) I can't bear him. I see my grandmother, she is scornful.

T. Listen to your grandmother's voice.

P. She is cold and aggressive, full of scorn.

T. What words does your grandmother say in her cold, aggressive voice?

P. 'Don't make such a fuss. (The next words) Pull yourself together. If you go with a man, it is only to be expected.' I see my mother crying. She is alone. I see my mother from above.

T. Tell me the words which drive you out of your body.

P. I can't bear it.

T. Listen again to what your grandmother says about 'going with men'.

P. Don't make such a fuss.

T. Tell me the words your mother is thinking.

P. How can she say that. After all I did love him. (The next words) I hate you.

T. What does your grandmother say to you and to your mother about men?

P. I can only see her lying in bed.

T. Tell me the first words which prevent you hearing what she says.

P. No, no, I can't bear it.

T. What does your mother feel in her body in connection with 'I can't bear it'.

P. The child wants to come out, she is helpless, she ought to push, but she holds back. She will not let go of the child.

T. What words might your mother say as she holds the child back?

P. After all, it is mine. It is the only thing I have. (The next words) I hate you all.

T. On which part of your mother's body are the words 'I hate you all' centred?

P. I see my head coming out.

T. Tell me the first words which make you come out of your body and observe yourself.

P. What an old hag that is with the apron on! What an aggressive situation there is here! The atmosphere is so aggressive, the voices are so loud and cold.

T. Pinpoint the loud voices in the room; are they coming from the left or the right?

P. One on the right, the other half right.

T. Male or female?

P. Female.

T. What are the first aggressive words which come up while you are being born.

P. Come on, come on, come on! Quick, quick. Hurry up. The baby is there.

T. When you hear the aggressive voices, which part of your body do you connect with them?

P. I'm cold, I'm frightened.

T. We will go back. Do you come out head first?

P. I think so.

T. What feeling do you have in your shoulders and your head as the head is coming out?

P. Relief.

T. What occurs to you next?

P. I'm glad that it is over.

T. Go back again to the momnent when you are leaving the womb.

P. It is a struggle.

T. Which part of your body is affected by it?

P. My head, there is pressure in my head as if I have to fight.

T. What words are connected with this?

P. A hectic atmosphere (What words?) Quick, come on, come on, hurry up. (The next words) The baby is suffocating. Hurry up!

T. What do you feel in your body?

P. I can't get enough air. I am frightened.

T. If someone in the room is making you say words of fear, who is it?

P. My grandmother.

T. What are the first words she says?

P. It is only a girl. (The next words) That is all you have managed.

T. What does she do to you now?

P. She takes me away.

T. Tell me all the words and unspoken things she has conveyed to you.

P. She says fine words, but in reality she despises me. Falsehood.

T. How does it feel not to be able to breathe yet?

P. Terrible.

T. What words would you say to people to indicate that you can't breathe yet?

P. Do help me! Come on, pull me out of here! I can't get any air. (The next words) Thank goodness, now I am out.

T. If someone other than yourself were to say these words, who could it be?

P. The midwife.

T. Pay attention to what the midwife is saying.

P. She is speaking calmly. 'It is all right.' the coldness comes from my grandmother. My mother is crying.

I need only consider what would have happened if I had left my client in the belief that she had hated her mother's body. It is impossible for a baby to hate anything at all, it has no conception of hate, it has nothing to hate with. We would only have increased her problem. One does that until the separation takes place. After that she could accept her own body. When my client was pregnant with her own child, all the hatred was activated. Her mother had not changed, but her attitude towards her mother had changed. After this session, I asked the patient how she felt. 'I see the connection between a hectic atmosphere, aggression and loud voices, which I cannot bear today. As far as food is concerned, it must be something rather different. I feel well and strong when I have eaten, I felt free. When I realised that my mother's thoughts in the second month were directed against her own body and not against me, I felt incredibly warm, I had a good feeling in my body, without any struggle. I used always to have a feeling that I must fight against everything.

Eating is possibly a compensation for the time from birth to being fed. 'When I eat I do not feel alone, abandoned, helpless.'

Since she had told me in the first session that her husband's aggressive voice induced her to eat, I knew that we had to look for an aggressive voice during the prenatal period or at the birth. If an aggressive voice is part of the problem, it will also be found in former lives.

Here is another example from my practice, in which condemning and judging play an important part. The client, who has already worked through some of his memories in earlier rebirthing sessions, and can relate to these, says in the first consultation about his problems:

'I have had a dramatic life. My mother wanted to kill me when I was three months old by pushing a pillow onto my face, but she did not succeed. I kept on accusing my mother until I saw that I was provoking her. I kept on screaming for three months until she blew a fuse. Now I would like to know where this "I can't trust anyone, I'll never trust anyone" comes from. I have learnt in life to trust people, but I've got an impression that in a former life someone whom I trusted betrayed me. My mother had several abortions before she had me.'

T. Concentrate on the feelings you connect with trust. Request your subconscious to find the traumatic moment before you were born. You have already found it. Tell me the first words that occur to you.

P. I want to get rid of this baby. May I do it? That's what I would like best. Whatever shall I do? I wish someone would help me.

T. Let your subconscious go to the moment before conception with the same mother, when these words were activated.

P. My God, I'm going to have a baby! I haven't got any money (Abortion) I shall be glad when it's over, I hope it will soon be over.

T. Tell me what physical attitude your mother is in when the abortion takes place.

P. She is in the medical practice, sitting on a woman's chair.

T. Is she alone?

P. The doctor is there.

T. What words do you hear?

P. It is finished.

T. What do you feel in the womb?

P. Nothing.

T. Go back to the moment when you felt something. Tell me what the doctor did first to terminate the pregnancy.

P. Someone is touching me, pulling me out.

T. Which part of your body would be affected if your body were already formed.

P. The head.

T. What is your mother thinking about it?

P. Thank goodness, that's over! Now I am happy. I shall never do that again.

T. Tell me the first words your mother is thinking when the doctor begins the intervention.

P. My goodness, I hope he will find it.

T. What words is she thinking about your death?

P. I'm glad it's over. I will never become pregnant again.

T. If you had made a promise to your mother at this point, what would have been your words?

P. I shall come again, I promise you, you will be my mother.

T. Go through your mother's thoughts again.

P. The baby is threatening my life. It's better for the child to die and for me to live. Someone is touching me. I can't trust anyone. They are against me. Here was the place to which I had a claim. I have killed my mother twenty times over in my thoughts. Leave me in peace! You have no right to do that to me. If I could, I would fight against you.

T. What feeling do you have when the doctor is pulling your head?

P. I am helpless. It depresses me to be helpless. I shall pay you back for it.

T. What words would you say to your mother at your death?

P. You have no idea what you are doing. You are stupid. If only I had time, I would explain it to you.

T. Go through it again.

P. Someone is stabbing me. My God!

T. Do you feel the dagger going through you?

P. It is going through my breast. (The next words) You? I can't believe that it is you. The dagger is going right through me. I am so surprised that I can't move.

T. Go back a little. What were you doing before you were stabbed?

P. There are a lot of people there, for whom I am responsible. I have made a lot of demands. I am wearing a red robe.

T. What did you demand of them?

P. I wanted them to be true to me.

T. What words did you say, before you were attacked?

P. I want you to follow me.

T. What words does the person with the dagger say?

P. I won't.

T. What do you say to him?

P. No, not you! You don't know what you are doing! You are making a mistake. I shall never forget it.

T. Pay attention to the promise you are making here.

P. I shall take it with me. It will never happen to me again. I cannot trust anyone. I fall backwards.

T. Pain?

P. No.

T. Words?

P. No.

T. What words does the person say or think, who has stabbed you?

P. I've done it. It is a misunderstanding. A saying of Steiner's occurs to me: 'The worst thing to reform is incompetence. I hate it when someone does something without being clear about the consequences.

T. With what words did you die?

P. I shall come again. I hate mistakes. That's why I always wanted to be perfect.

T. How does the previous life tie up with your birth?

P. I thought, this time it will be all right. I shall make it. (He breathes deeply)

T. If someone is breathing deeply, who is it?

P. My mother.

T. What is she thinking?

P. I want it to be over soon. I must go on breathing. I keep telling the people that! At birth the navel cord was cut, I didn't want that. I felt it was a betrayal.

Wrong judgments, too quickly made, command our attention and prevent rational thinking. A decision, once made, can be altered only when a person finds the reason for that decision and changes it into a rational, open point of view. In the first example from my practice, the client in the womb had wrongly taken her mother's rejection of her own body to be her mother's rejection of the client herself.

The second example is interlarded with valuations, judgments, condemnations, decisions and executions. It says there: 'I am glad it's over. I will never become pregnant again.' Here is a valuation resulting in a decision, meaning pregnancy brings pain, it hurts me, I will not allow it any more. Such a decision can result in this person remaining childless in a later life, although there is an urgent longing for a child. The incarnating soul also made a decision, 'You will be my mother'. Here two conflicting decisions come one after the other and this forms a basis for the most conflict-laden relationship between mother and child. The mother thinks: 'The child shall die and I will live.' This can lead to losing the child later through death. The client says: 'I have killed my mother twenty times over in my thoughts.' That is an execution. 'I must not trust' is a valuation.

I would like here to emphasise the importance of decisions, valuations, judgments and condemnations which happen in the mind since they have a tendency to materialise in some way or another. It is not fate, as is generally supposed, which makes one's life difficult. It is, above all, the decisions one makes oneself, for from them arises what we call fate. So if one wants to understand and change one's fate, one must first of all discover one's own decisions, which fate is obeying. In Rudolf Steiner's book *Theosophy* in the last chapter, called *The Path of Perception*, there are fundamental words about the consequences of judgment: 'What has been said already hints at a quality which a person must first develop in himself if he wants to arrive at his own perception of higher facts. It is unreserved and dispassionate submission to what is revealed by human life and also by the world outside man. The learner must at all times be able to make himself an empty vessel, into which the outside world will flow. The only moments of perception are those where every judgment, every criticism proceeding from is is silent. Anyone wishing to tread the higher path of perception must practise being able at any moment to obliterate himself, with all his prejudices. As long as he obliterates himself, the other will flow into him. This dispassionate submission has nothing whatever to do with blind faith. It is not a question of believing blindly in something, but of not putting "blind judgment" in the place of a living impression.'

In all ages the great teachers of truth saw themselves faced with a mighty question: how can the human mind learn the truth, which will set it free? At a cursory glance you might think that this was only a question of time and that, through his manifold experiences, a person would, in the normal course of things, develop further. Looked at more closely, however, it turns out that, in spite of all their efforts, many people do not progress any further. They have visited doctors, psychotherapists and spiritual teachers in the hope of obtaining help from them; but we do not obtain real help until we decide to do something ourselves towards our inward liberation.

If someone wants to develop himself further and choses, for example, RT as his way, he should bring with him a few prerequisites. He should have a genuine desire for change. A further principle is that he should trust RT. If he criticises and doubts, he will only hinder himself. The third point is to be honest with himself. This honesty requires him to be open to new perceptions about himself. Further development also means freeing oneself from a wrong idea of one's own worth, since new perceptions cannot arise without a certain amount of disillusionment and the relinquishing of old values. One has first to make room for them. The last point is endurance and perseverence. No therapy can solve, in a week or in a month, all the problems which have existed for a whole lifetime. For reincarnation therapists as well, their work requires much sympathetic understanding and attention to detail.

Let us examine these points rather more closely.

There may be a wish for change, but real change does not come until inward thoughts and desires have changed. It is a mistake to think that the world around us must change first, before we ourselves can be happy. 'If only other people were not so hard and selfish, then I would not have to suffer like this.' 'If only my husband were more understanding, we would get on together much better.' 'If only my boss was not always so unkind, I would not have to be afraid of having made a mistake.'

These are a few examples of expectations people have of the world around them. RT proceeds on the assumption that everything we meet is a mirror of ourselves or a challenge to get to grips with something. If we were honest about our own fate, we should have to say, 'What is it in me which is not yet mature, not sufficiently transparent, which makes life confront me continually with these problems? What am I doing in my life to attract this fate and what should I learn from it?'

Most of these questions can be answered only by means of our previous lives. In order that there may be a change in our life, we must accept these with all that that entails and be ready to reshape our life.

This may mean giving up many long-established habits and activities, if these are no longer useful, in order to make way for new activities and views. it takes courage to do this – and one shows courage by being honest about oneself. A courageous person will put up with being laughed at, criticised or rejected by the world around him, as long as he knows in himself that he is right. Nothing is of greater worth for a person than to be honest with himself. With this quality, every obstacle in life can be overcome. A person, who is not honest with himself, will also tend to distrust others. In this way he diverts attention from his own uncertainty and projects negative qualities into the world around him. Problems cannot be solved on this basis, since the person in question is looking for the cause in the world around him and not in himself.

6.

The Practical Application of Reincarnation Therapy

Christian Morgenstern writes in his *Steps*: 'Each illness has its own particular sense, since each illness is a purification, but one has to find out what it is a purification of. There is reliable information about this, but people prefer to read and think about hundreds and thousands of matters, which do not concern them, rather than about their own affairs. They do not want to learn how to read the profound hieroglyphs of their illnesses and are more interested in the playthings of life than in its seriousness. The real reason why their illnesses are not cured lies in lack of perception and aversion to it, rather than in bacteria.'

When purification is mentioned this means that not only what is faulty must be overcome, but also what is old, what has become obsolete right back to a former life. It must be sloughed off like an old skin. Seen in this way, an illness can serve the purpose of sloughing a skin of the soul.

Self-discovery, self-realisation is one of the central themes of psychologists, educational theorists and sociologists. Everyone agrees that it is difficult for a person to find himself. But what is it that makes this process so difficult? Are the hindrances more outward or more inward ones? Sociologists and often educational theorists seek the chief factors in disturbances mainly in the outward conditions of social, professional and family life. But is it not the person himself, who is the greatest hindrance in this life process? How can the forces of self development be released in a person who imagines that he has been 'ready' for a long time? How can a person find himself, if he does not seek himself? There are people who reach the age of seventy or eighty without having ever in their lives asked the question 'who am I really?' They appear to be without any problems, quite naively at home in themselves without ever having been disturbed by this feeling of their own identity. The idea of someone suddenly waking up as though from a dream and not knowing who he is, seems absurd. But we are not only the person whose life we are living; we are also the person we once were. And this identification of oneself from a previous life can have a most disturbing effect on our present life. So it is important to learn to distinguish between present thoughts and emotions and those of a former life.

That is also the reason why, before embarking on reincarnation experiences, we first work through the difficulties and traumas of the present life. Various things must be worked through, for example serious operations, war experiences, dangerous situations, shocks, etc. Such experiences are worked through by the technique of regression, like this: Now we are going to the beginning of your operation. You are already there. Tell me your first impressions. Where are you? What do you see? What do you feel? What is happening to you after the anaesthetic has been administered? What is the doctor doing, what is being said? Tell the dialogue word for word. If your consciousness were not dulled by the anaesthetic, what pain would you feel in your body at this moment?

Each trauma is thoroughly worked through, until all suggestive effects of the words spoken during the operation have been removed and the contents are known. When all the difficulties of the present life have been worked through, we go into the so-called prenatal phase in order to work through all the disturbing conditions during pregnancy. I say: 'We will now make contact with the nine months of pregnancy. Everything was registered in your sub-conscious. Say the number of one of the months of pregnancy from one to nine. In this month your mother was concerned with a problem. Say the first words that come to mind. What is your mother thinking, what is she feeling at this moment? What problem came up during pregnancy for your mother or for your father?' If there are quarrels we will switch in to the dialogue: 'Listen to what your mother is saying. What is she saying, what does her voice sound like? What is the other person saying? Who is the other person? What does your mother think in the first moment about being pregnant? What does your father say about it?'

Decisive, emotionally coloured situations during pregnancy are discussed. 'We will now go into your birth. How do you feel? What is the position of your body? When the birth process begins, what do you feel in your body? What changes are setting in? How do you react to them? What do you feel when you enter the birth canal? Admit to all the feelings you have in your body, describe them. Listen to the words outside, what is being said. What is your mother doing, what is she saying? What does the doctor, the midwife say? What do you feel when the birth is over and you are out? What happens after that?'

'We will now make contact with a past life, which caused your present problem. Your sub-conscious knows this life, knows the root of your problems today. Say the first words that come to mind.' If people say: 'I don't feel anything; I can't feel my body', this means the same as: 'I can't hear/see anything.' 'What has happened to you that is blocking your feeling? Are you paralysed, is your spine broken? Were you given any medicine? What has happened to block any feeling of your body?' Even if feeling of the body is impeded, it is still possible to arrive at these feelings during therapy. The greatest blockage is 'I don't know.'

'I don't know' is an incomplete answer. I do not accept it. If a patient says 'I don't know', I assume that he is already inside the event and that 'I don't know' is already a part of his answer. If 'I don't know' comes from the prenatal phase, I say: 'Tell me the rest of the sentence, what does your mother not know? Do not stop at "I don't know". "I don't know, I don't know" . . . The first words that occur to you'. 'I don't know what I am to do with this man all my life. . . '

There is also another possibility: 'If you knew it, what do you think it would be.' That breaks through the resistance. There are people who think first and people who feel first. As a therapist, one very quickly finds this out. You cannot tell someone to feel the picture first, when he has to see it first. That will not work. After a patient has lived through an event, you make him go through the same event again until the trauma has disappeared and he can go through it easily. After he has gone through it a second time, I ask: 'Are you in some way physically or emotionally tied to the trauma?' If there is still something there, he will tell me. I do not need to decide whether the experience is now closed, I only have to be in a position to ask the client. We are not omniscient and we cannot get into the skin of another person. Our main rule is: I will take whatever the patient offers me and work through it, until it is no longer a problem. The client will tell me exactly what I need to know.

By this method, the subconscious will find the most intense

trauma, which has to be worked through. When you work through this event, a whole series of similar experiences is explained. If the event is not resolved, you go back further, but this is not automatic procedure. You request the subconscious to seek out the experience, which will solve the problem.

Experiences in former lives are not more important or more intense than experiences in this life. If you have any myths or illusions in this connection, rid yourself of them. The mysterious aura surrounding previous lives comes from an attempt to furnish a proof, which we do not do. We act on the premise that previous lives represent a reality.

Part of the subconscious always knows what is happening, even under hypnosis, the 'eternal witness'. You can ask the patient: 'Part of you knows what is happening. Tell me the first thing that occurs to you.' This is especially helpful when the patient is confused. Confusion is the last defence put up to conceal pain. The therapist should not be disturbed by confusion, it will be treated just like everything else. If someone says: 'I am so confused, I simply don't know. . .', I say: 'Good, there is a reason why you are confused. Tell me the first words which come to you, which are causing your confusion.'

If a patient comes to the practice with a dangerous complaint, such as heart attacks, you should not immediately begin with the subject 'heart attacks', or he might have an attack during the therapy. I ask what stresses there were in his life, when the heart attacks began and work through these. Sooner or later the answer to his illness will come up, but in a way which the patient himself will accept and he will be able to go on living in spite of it. Heart attacks are only the symptoms of a problem; stress produces the attack. If we trace this back to former lives, we shall find perhaps a spear through the heart in a desperate situation. If we go back to more primitive times, the causes of the pain will also be primitive, a spear or a rock may be the cause.

The patient is not allowed to discuss his experiences or just to recall them, he must relive them. If he evades it, I bring him back.

The therapist's voice must be definite and he should speak in the present tense: 'Where are you when the telephone rings, bringing you the news of your daughter's accident? With which hand are you taking off the receiver? What does the caller say? What is your first reaction when you hear these words? What are you thinking? What are you saying?'

Traumas from this life must be worked through first, before concerning oneself with those in former lives. I had a client with a drink problem, who suffered from too close a bond with his mother and had problems with his wife. At the age of four he had had to undergo an operation on his ear. I decided to work through this operation, since most of the decisions about this life are made at the age of three to six years. Every word spoken by the doctor or the nurse while he is under anaesthetic will be part of the client's later motivation.

P. I felt alone after the operation. My mother could come only every second day.

T. Were you prepared for the operation?

P. No.

T. Act on the assumption that you know everything; what happened, what was said, everything that happened outside, while the operation was going on. Your subconscious knows it – we will now go into this section of your life.

You are four years old. Tell me the first thing that occurs to you to connect us with the operation on your ear. Tell me the first place that occurs to you, when you were in the hospital.

P. My ear hurts.

T. Concentrate on the pain in your ear. Can you hear anything at all that the people around you are saying? The first words which occur to you.

P. I can't hear anything.

T. If there were anyone there saying that you cannot hear, tell me the first words which occur to you which this person would be saying.

P. We must hurry up. We must perform the operation today. Prepare the operation. Take him to the operating theatre. It feels as though my head is bursting.

T. What is happening to you externally? Are you being wheeled along? What is the first thing which happens to you? Has the anaesthetic injection already been given to you? Yes or no?

P. Yes.

T. Tell me the first words said when you are given the injection.

P. It won't hurt at all. Keep quite calm, I am with you.

T. What do you feel in your hands and feet.

P. Coldness.

T. What do they do to you, when you have received the injection?

P. I don't know what they are going to do to me.

T. If you were able to ask, what would you ask?

P. What are you going to do to me? Will it hurt me? I want to go to my mother. Let my mother come here, tell her to be with me. Help me. I feel so helpless. I can't feel my ear.

T. Are you still in bed or on the operating table?

P. Op. table. Now I am getting the gas mask.

T. When you feel something covering your nose, what are the first words you would like these people to say?

P. Take it away! Where is my mother?

T. What do you feel, when you are breathing?

P. Tiredness.

T. Tell me the words the people say which have something to do with your tiredness.

P. Can you count? 1, 2, 3, 4, 5, 6. . .

T. What happens to your body when you reach 6? What effect does the counting have on you?

P. I become unconscious.

T. If someone were to say something about your not hearing, what would he say? The people in op. go on talking. If someone were to speak, where would this person be standing, at the head or the foot, on the right or the left?

P. At the head.

T. A male or female voice?

P. Female.

T. Tell me the first words this female voice is saying. If she says 'He is sleeping, he is unconscious, he can't hear anything', don't obey her words, say the words out loud. (Pause) In what bodily position are you?

P. I am lying down.

T. What is happening to your right ear?

P. There is a terrible noise. I can't imagine what it is.

T. These are not your words. Who is saying these words? A man or a woman?

P. A man, the doctor.

T. What is he talking about, what is he doing while he is saying these words?

P. He is opening up the bone. 'It was high time. Tomorrow would have been too late. As it is, he will live. He will hear badly'.

T. You do not need to cling to these words. Let go of these words.

P. I am so tired.

T. Who is saying that?

P. The doctor.

T. Let go of these words.

P. Tell the mother that the child is all right. Ring me if anything happens.

T. What happens to you now?

P. I am back in the room.

T. Is anything else said?

P. I have a son like that too. I will look after him.

T. Does this woman tell you any news?

P. She is only looking after me.

T. When you wake up, is something being said around you?

P. I want to go to my mother, where is my mother, I want to go home. Perhaps I am going to die. I can't live without my mother. I don't understand why she is not with me. It feels as if my ear had been cut off. Give me back my ear.

T. Make yourself fully aware again that your mother is not there. If you were to promise her something at this moment, if only she were with you and she would not leave you alone in this place, where you may be going to die, what would you promise?

P. I will marry you.

T. What happens when you see your mother again after the operation?

P. My mother has been crying.

Subsequent Consultation

T. Now that you are an adult, what must you do after having made that promise to your mother? You were given something to deaden your consciousness. Now you are married. When you needed a wife at four years old, she was not there. Now you need something to suppress your fears – alcohol. Just as at that time you were given something to deaden your consciousness, alcohol means for you today 'becoming unconscious', the possibility of withdrawing from aggression against your wife and the stress connected with it.

Sentences with the force of a suggestion which are spoken, for example, during operations or during birth, such as 'You can't remember', lodge in the subconscious the conflict of not being allowed or supposed to do something which has, however, already happened. The 'not remembering' here covers up the memory, which is still there and is just being screened off.

All sentences containing 'not' programme the contents without the 'not'. When thinking positively, one should not say 'I will never be ill again' or 'I will never strain myself again', because here again the negative element is suggested to the sub conscious. Instead, one should use sentences such as 'I am well', 'I am relaxed.'

Many people believe that because they can make people experience a former life, they would be able to practise reincarnation therapy. That is not true. There is no art in making someone experience a former life. Any non-therapist can do it with a few simple questions, but the important thing is to work at the traumas thoroughly for long enough for them no longer to be a problem.

I have no fear of treating screaming and raving patients. The therapist must be free enough to let the patients express themselves in this way. I must locate the trauma, go into it, let them relive it and finish with it. There is nothing frightening about that, if I just let it happen. Many people want to check such a reaction, there are even some forms of therapy, which block off any contact with traumas. In order to be effective in this therapy, many people will have to give up their desire to be in control. A person who feels the need to control everything around him cannot become a reincarnation therapist.

The basic cause of suppressed memories lies in earlier pain and trauma which were not resolved. The reason this problem exists in the here and now is that the memory is activated on an unconscious level. The memory contains unresolved traumas; or else one is simply incapable of recognising that the event is over. Details, such as times, places, names etc do not normally come to light. If someone is interested in this information, he should tell me in advance, so that I can specifically ask questions about it.

I do absolutely nothing in order to obtain the information, except to work with what the client has told me. In hypnotherapy a procedure is applied in order to induce the hypnosis. There is scarcely a single hypnotherapist who can leave his own aims and objects and suggestions out of the process. I give my clients no points of reference, I work only with the data they have given me.

Just a word about fantasy. I have never met pure fantasy. It is always based in some way on reality. Many people say: 'It's just my imagination'. That is correct. Imagination is a synthesis of all that has ever happened to a person; it includes every former life. All fantasy is based on reality. If you trace the fantasy back to a body which has physical reality, then fantasy ceases to be fantasy.

Material from former lives is dramatic and traumatic and many clients think it would be too much for them. Here the therapist must convince the client. One can go back infinitely far in time without finding a point where memory ends; but therapy seems to limit itself to the level of the earth. Life on other planets is not ruled out, but often people do not find themselves on Mars or Venus, as they perhaps had assumed, but on Atlantis. People like to perceive themselves as human beings; what is much more difficult for them is to recognise themselves in stages of animal development. On the animal level there is instinct, not the capacity to think and to rationalise.

If you transpose yourself to that level, you will see that it is here that the origins of some problems are to be found. The instinct of self preservation, territorial delineation and reproduction – all areas of present day life – had their origins at animal level.

In our earlier lives many and various experiences will be found, but in therapy one first defines the present problem and concentrates the regressing on this until it has been solved. Therapy orientates itself on the problem. The level above the animal level corresponds to the prenatal phase, the animal level and a little above or below it corresponds to former lives. Human problems begin in the middle phase, when one emerges from the cave period and enters the tribal period. Here the outside world is trying to tell us how we should solve our problems and how we should conform.

Often the life immediately before this one acts as a hub around which all problems rotate. If one concentrates on this previous life and works with it alone, whole ranges of problems can be solved; normally, one works where the patient's subconscious directs. We return the problem to the patient as he originally described it to us and let his subconscious pinpoint the spots where we must work.

The language used in RT is not exactly what you might expect. We avoid such expressions as 'Go back to . . . Look for and find . . .', because they place the subconscious in a seeking position. We say: 'You are already there. You have just found it.

You have just got there, now tell me the first words which occur to you, which connect us with the event. You have just found it, what are the first words which occur to you?'

The client's first words will be judged as his answer, they already present part of the problem. If the client says: 'I don't know', I accept that this is his answer to my question.

Sometimes fixed assumptions exist as to what a former life is and what it should be like. In many cases you have first to alter these assumptions. Sometimes I wish that people would not believe in reincarnation at all, since their fixed assumptions are often hard to overcome. It is often easier to work with people who do not believe in anything, but are prepared to try out this therapy.

The best way to begin is to work with the prenatal phase and to define the problem. As soon as every trauma in this sphere has been worked through, I ask the client to let his subconscious go back to an earlier event, which forms the connection with the prenatal phase. After I have worked through this experience, there follows a further step to the next experience, which is necessary in order to overcome the problem. The answers then form a complete picture, furnished by the client's subconscious. It contains nothing suggested by the therapist. All I have done is to ask the client to regress.

He may, perhaps, say to me: 'I can't walk, I can't move.' When I have brought the client to the point of describing his feelings in sentences, then the real work of the session can begin.

If I hear a sentence like 'I can't move', I let the client repeat it several times. Repetition draws the client into the experience and keeps him there. At the first repetition, the statement is localised, at the second it is heard and at the third it is consciously duplicated.

Most compulsions and phobias are only a cloak for something else. If I suspect this, I say to the patient: 'Shut your eyes. At some time during the prenatal phase, something happened to your mother which is causing you this problem today.' If the patient has difficulties: 'You have just located the trauma. Name any month during pregnancy, from nought to nine. The first month which comes into your head.'

'The fourth.'

'The cause of your present problem lies somewhere in the fourth month. You are now in connection with this problem from the prenatal period. Tell me the first words of your mother which occur to you and which will connect us with the trauma of the fourth month.'

Even that can lead the therapist astray. A client will not relinquish his problem. He cannot solve it and reports the same problem over a long period. When I see that the therapy is getting nowhere, I leave off the therapy which has been pursued so far and look for the 'endless' sentence, a sentence which is continual. If his mother, during her pregnancy with her thirteenth child, says: 'Do what I will, it never gets any better' and the thirteenth child is my patient, I must first extract this material from the subconscious, otherwise nothing I am doing will lead anywhere. This programme can have devastating results on the life of my client: 'Never mind what I do. . .'

'Endless' sentences contain words with a boundless idea of time, 'never', 'never again', 'ever', 'always', etc. 'How shall I ever get on with this man?' 'I shall never understand that', 'However much trouble you take, you never get anything given to you', 'Whatever happens, I shall never forget that', etc. These sentences act as a programme, and because there is no limit to how long it may last, the subconscious will go on obeying it until the programme is consciously ended.

There is another reason for stubborn problems. Every irrationality, every illness was at some time to the advantage of the person concerned, otherwise he would not go on reproducing this situation. The problem is useful for the patient. 'If I am ill, other people will look after me', 'As long as I am weak, no one can hold me responsible', 'As long as I have problems, my partner cannot leave me'. Here you must find out the calculation which has been made and lay bare the advantages quite clearly and it will turn out that the problem originally stated was not the real one at all, but only an alibi problem. The real problem may be dread of responsibility, fear of being left alone or inability to fulfil one's own needs. As long as the therapist is treating the 'wrong' problem, there can be no change in the client's condition.

Sometimes, when the patient is questioned about the origin of the problem, apparently positive experiences will come up, as in the case of one client, who always first saw herself going down a river in a boat, with no problems, no trauma, nothing at all. Finally I asked her: 'Can you tell me the first reason which occurs to you, why your subconscious should have chosen out this occurrence?' Her answer was simply: 'I would rather go downstream in a boat than be bound to the stake.' 'Aha! What stake?' 'Oh, the one in another life, which caused me so much pain.'

We found out that she had died as a martyr at the stake and had cried out before her death: 'Let me out of here! Please make the pain stop! Let me go!' In the session she had obeyed her own words and gone into a life in which there was no pain. The subconscious obeys the first orders in the occurrence. This patient had been burnt as a witch in another life and had sworn never to be a woman again. If I am not a woman, I cannot be a witch. She had kept her promise – in the subsequent lives she had always been a man. This was the first life after being burnt in which she was a woman again.

In the case of homosexuality, it often happens that something terrible occurred in a former life, so that, for example, the person swears: 'I will never be a woman again', but is now trying to solve the feminine problem in her role as a man.

Unfortunately there is no simple rule for treating homosexuals, but some confusion of the role of the sexes is always present. You are most certain to proceed when you trace back traumas in the role of both sexes, since obviously avoidance of the role of one of the sexes is present. Guilt towards the other sex can also cause a homosexual tendency. If a man has oppressed and tortured women in one life, he may want to avoid encountering women in the role of a man in the next life. His bad conscience tells him it would be better to keep away from women. Should the same former male oppressor be born as a woman in the next life, this woman may want to keep away from men, since men are horrid and evil and only want to harm you. This woman is in the present projecting her own male past on to the whole male sex.

Another problem which may present itself, is when you go far back into the past, where there is no speech. The patient sees himself as a hairy being sitting round a fire, but is unable to express himself in speech. Here I ask: 'If you were able to speak, what would be the first words you would say?' This also applies to foreign languages. If someone speaks a foreign language in a session: 'Then you spoke a foreign language, but today you speak German. Please translate.' It may happen that a patient will speak a foreign language fluently in the session, which he has never learnt in this life and which he does not understand either. This happens from time to time, but has no significance for the therapy itself.

Somatic troubles can be brought to an end by this therapy,

provided the therapist always takes care that the patient remains inside his body during regression. Strong emotions are the remains of physical traumas, which the therapist seeks out in the following way: if the client has strong anger or fear, he asks: 'In which part of your body is this anger, this fear situated?' 'Which physical feeling comes up?' 'Pain'. 'In which part of your body is this pain?' 'In my heart.' 'What is happening to your heart, tell me the first thing which occurs to you.'

Another way of tackling problems is as follows: I trace the chain of occurrences back and work through the experiences. If there were not something left unsolved in the occurrence, it would not trouble the person concerned today. After the trauma has been worked through, I ask about the problem which is left unsolved at the end of that life. Then I say: 'Go now into an occurrence closer to the present, in which you tried to find an answer to this problem, to solve it.' I work through this occurrence and then ask about the problem left unsolved at the end of this life, go nearer to the present again and find the next experience when the client tried to solve this question, and so on right up to the present life. Here I ask what question the person brought with him into the prenatal phase, then I go into the birth ('Tell me the first thing which occurs to you, when you tried to answer this question at your birth'). I reach the here and now, where the question is usually solved.

I am frequently asked how it is that through the population explosion there are four thousand million people living on the earth. Where do all these souls come from? From the practice of reincarnation therapy, I can answer this by saying that during the last 3,000 years souls have been incarnating more quickly than they did before that. The phase between lives has, on the average, become shorter and shorter, presumably because in the age of Aquarius there are intensive possibilities for further development, of which the souls want to make use. Also there is probably no static number of souls present on the level of the earth, because new ones arrive and old ones, who have surmounted the earth level, find themselves on a higher level of consciousness and do not incarnate any more.

In many estoteric schools there are fixed opinions about the number of earth lives, about the length of time in the phases between lives and about the division of life between the female and male sexes. In practice, no one has been able to demonstrate any fixed rule. The number of earth lives goes into thousands, the phases between lives are of the most varied lengths and the change from one sex to another does not follow any definite sequence.

Now and then the fear is expressed that solving old problems would turn a person into an emotional neuter, that he would lose his individuality. The case is exactly the opposite – old programmes make people alike, they have similar fears and behavioural patterns. True individuality succeeds in reaching full development only when the unconscious programming is removed. A further field, with which we must occupy ourselves, is critical illnesses and their psychological treatment. We must have the conviction that we are well able to govern our own bodies, that we act in a causal capacity in relation to them. The therapist must believe this himself, but he must also convince his patients of it. He cannot heal his patient's body with his own power, but with the patient's power. We go back and find the cause of this illness, eg an occurrence in the patient's life which has caused him hopelessness, helplessness, specifically six months to two years before the outbreak of the illness. Then we go back and find the causes in the precise part of the body in which, for example, the cancer is situated, that is to say in the prenatal phase and in previous lives. Then I ask the patient to write down five advantages which the illness brings him. Normally patients will dispute the idea that illness brings any advantage at all, but they soon observe that, for example, through their illness they are able for the first time to express their feelings for their loved ones or the other way round, they now allow themselves to rest, which they never did before, or they are more creative than before.

Thus the illness has its uses. The next step is to help the patient to find ways and means of satisfying these same needs without the illness. At the same time, during therapy, I carry out exercises in imagination with the patient. He imagines his body healthy and well. There are some schools which do this by means of brutal mental images, eg soldiers fighting the cancer or wild dogs eating up the cancer, but violent images only cause more pain. I let my patient imagine his body healthy with a strong heart pumping healthy, healing blood through his body. However, as long as the patient still feels helpless and powerless, imagination cannot work. For this reason it is important to overcome helplessness and lack of courage by going back through the prenatal period and former lives, until I find out what their cause is.

The prerequisites on the part of the client are that he should be open and ready to accept all the consequences of working on himself. He should also have tried to solve his problems himself, before seizing on a therapy. Pure curiosity is not a good basis, although behind so-called curiosity there is often a wish to find out more about oneself and this in its turn completely justifies using a therapy.

A prerequisite for the therapist is to have had therapy himself, since this protects him from being restimulated by his client's events. Only a therapist with a neutral attitude can safely lead a client through his traumas and see through his avoidance mechanisms. Until the therapist has solved his own fundamental range of problems, he will attract clients with similar ones and he will not be sufficiently unprejudiced to apply himself to these problems. RT is a fundamental and relentless therapy. Only someone who has confronted himself with his former lives and has thereby re-experienced all levels of human existence is in a position to bring others through their own conflicts and the experiences which they try to avoid.

By working through former lives, one immediately touches on the core of life's difficulties, and therefore changes very quickly appear for the client. It may happen that, after as little as two or three sessions, basic conflicts or vital questions will be solved.

Other ranges of problems may take rather longer and require new life situations to be experienced. Life matches our state of consciousness exactly and presents us with just the situation we need in order to advance further. Thus, it may happen that during regressions a client speaks of his 'fear of confined spaces' and on the following day he becomes shut in the lift. Here fate is giving him the opportunity of tackling this problem anew and of consciously living through the reactions connected with it.

The more aware we become, the greater the tasks which life will set us. During and after therapy, changes come – new places of work, new spheres of activity are offered us, our relationship with our partner proceeds on a different level, new interests are wakened. There may also be crises if these are necessary for the process of maturing, until the period of adjustment is over. If we are ready for a change and have not yet recognised this ourselves and have not taken the necessary steps, the world around us will be hostile towards us. It will want to be rid of us, because it feels that we no longer belong in this environment. An employee suddenly gets into difficulties at his place of work, he simply cannot manage his job any longer and his colleagues and the world around reject him. This may be the result of his inward desire for change, for example setting up on his own. Since he does not make a move himself, fate forces him to leave the old sphere and apply himself to new tasks. Shortly before birth, a baby may feel that its mother's body is hostile because it wants to be free of the baby and pushes it out. However in reality the stage of development in its mother's body is now finished and the baby must become independent, whether it likes it or not. If a person has grown out of a stage of development, an activity or a relationship and has not yet realised this, the old situation will through a growing unpleasantness become untenable and will fall apart. Instead of complaining about losses and crises, we should rather look on fate as our friend. We should see the crisis as the last possibility of helping us to make progress after we our-selves have failed to make an effort at the right time to change ourselves. For this reason, it is necessary to have discussions after regressions in order to talk over with the client the changes which are occurring.

Every objection which a patient makes against a therapy shows up the client's personal problem. If someone makes the objection that he is too critical and lays too much stress on reason, then this person will have constructed this very mecha-nism of critical thinking based on reason in order to deal better with his problem. If someone is afraid that he may not be able to cope with what happens in therapy, then he will not be able to cope with situations in his present life, they will overwhelm him. People carry over the problem they have in life into their therapy. 'My reason is too strongly marked', can be translated as 'I don't want to encounter the sensitive, unconscious side of my personality yet, I don't feel equal to it.' It is not right to accuse reason of acting as a block. Reason has absolutely no interest in blocking us; it functions in accordance with its own laws. People like to use it as an excuse for not having to occupy themselves with the unconscious side of their personality.

In the course of therapy, a person becomes more and more himself, he finds the way back to his natural identity by parting from old identities. He becomes spontaneous, lives in the present, has a more realistic view of life and, at the same time, has at his disposal a heightened potential for creativity and imagination. The gap between reason and intuitive feeling disappears. He again becomes conscious of his full responsibility and the freedom which is connected with it and he is able to act in a sensitive manner, without harming himself and other people. Since, by re-experiencing all possible circumstances of life and levels of consciousness, he no longer has any resistance to difficult life situations or the negative parts of his own character, he is free to turn to any level of consciousness and to develop all his capacities. Problems can be tackled by acting them out; hindrances can be regarded as challenges to creativity and love of life returns. Nothing in life can cause him real fear or uneasiness and unpleasant things can be seen as aids and indications. Since he regards himself as the cause of his fate, he can have a constructive effect on that fate and spontaneously introduce necessary changes.

7.

Crises in Life and how they Manifest

Crises may manifst in a variety of ways, but more important than their differences is what they have in common. In every case, the person concerned is trying to protect his own life, is avoiding having to feel the pain of his experiences, whether it is a question of not loving one's partner, of not being loved by him, or of not wanting to accept a feeling of jealousy. Or it may be a question of a dawning realisation that his life up to now has been lived not in reality but in imagination, or it may be that in the struggle for recognition he has not been fair to himself and to his partner. It is always a question of a painful experience and of avoiding that experience.

What all crises have in common is avoidance of one's own painful experiences; the variety lies in the ways in which people avoid them. This can be by means of alcoholism, drugs, pills, becoming a 'workaholic' and many other strategies. The most decisive feature of all these evasive tactics is that they are not a means of satisfying needs, but rather a means of suppressing needs. There is much evidence to indicate that crises are a rebellion against the demand to be a person one is not. Particularly in a crisis in middle life, someone will suddenly and for no apparent reason fail in his profession or in his relations with his partner.

The things which stand out clearly in crises in one's life are fixed ideas and images of oneself, which bear the stamp of a former life, for example, the fixed idea that one must at all costs be liked and accepted by everyone. In that case behind all one's actions there will be the motivation of wanting to be on good terms with everyone. However this happens to the cost of one's own personality. It often turns out that the reason for this is that in a former life this person was accused, driven out or despised, so that not being accepted by other people spells danger, unpleasantness or death. This must at all costs be avoided in his later life and so arises the demand he makes on himself, which can never completely be realised, of wanting to be on good terms with everyone. As long as he can obey this demand, he feels safe; but if this demand is threatened by fate, ie the source from which he has previously drawn his recognition dries up, which may happen in the case of a separation or of being given notice, the image he has of himself is shaken and he goes into a crisis. His soul has not yet realised that the reason for the need to be recognised no longer exists in his present life and it lives according to a way of conduct belonging to its former life. However this hinders progress in the present life. It is necessary to find out the previous decisions and to resolve them in order to let the ego develop. On the other hand there may be tendencies, which are being rejected on account of a former decision, such as, for example, healthy egoism. If a person had too good a time in former lives, he may later make the decision to subordinate his own needs in future. However he does not always succeed in this and at times he may fall back into his old behaviour. He is then the one who is most shocked at himself and again there is the danger of a crisis.

One could state as a basic principle that a crisis is always a sign that a tendency which rightly belongs to someone is being allowed too little scope or is being suppressed or that a tendency which does not rightly belong to someone is being overindulged. Sooner or later this can no longer be maintained, the protective mechanism breaks down and many values come into question. Clinging to circumstances which have long been superseded, or failure to achieve one's own aims, also lead to conflict. Thus a person may not have recognised that what he has achieved so far in his profession is exhausted, since the tasks connected with it no longer give him the possibility of growth and he misses the opportunity of finding a new sphere of activity. Sooner or later his work will appear to him as senseless, he will make mistakes, he is no longer introducing anything creative and this sphere of work will somehow come to an end. In a love relationship, too, people can miss the opportunity of taking the next step in the relationship and, instead of that, cling to their old habits. Boredom, thoughts about separation and indifference are here just signs that both partners have not made their relationship sufficiently active and creative and have stuck to their usual relations with each other. Suppressed, forgotten and unachieved goals often form the basis of many substitute actions in life, which are not, however, entirely able to blot out the real goal. Unused gifts, talents, educational targets and fields of activity create a vacuum in the personality, which at some time later in life will appear in substitute form as discontent, emptiness, foolishness and inferiority. Every person has the task of making as good a use as possible of his potential. If he does not do so, then this will be seen as failure and he will wonder why he gets into a crisis. Time plays no part in this, a goal suppressed at the age of 20 may in some cases only reappear in the form of a crisis when the person is 50 years old. Of course it is not possible simply to achieve later every goal which has been suppressed, but it is sufficient to understand the connections and either knowingly to give up the old goal or if it is possible, to achieve this old goal. In a crisis, you can ask yourself: what is there in my life which is out of date, which no longer applies to me, to which I am still clinging?

Which of my needs have I not satisfied? To which tendencies have I not paid sufficient attention? Where have I underrated myself and my ability?

What am I doing in my life which I basically do not want? Where am I thinking I must do something, although I would not do it willingly? What possibilities do I have to release myself from this, so that I can get on with the things I really want to do instead? What have I failed to do so far in life, and what possibilities are there of attending to these things now?

People in a crisis are an annoyance to others and sometimes to themselves as well. Up to that point one could predict almost with certainty how a person would behave in a particular situation. Even he himself could say it of his own accord. Then suddenly these predictions no longer have a firm basis. Many people find this frightening and chaotic. Someone whose behaviour and reactions are predictable, has an image of himself which he is trying to realise. Someone who demands of himself that he should be such-and-such, reduces his experience to those elements which are reconcilable with that demand. That makes him predictable. Apparently, he himself can also trust himself. Apparently, because while he is striving to be what he thinks he ought to be, he is suppressing all the needs, feelings, efforts and experiences which would be in conflict with his image of himself. With every passing day, he is inwardly piling up more and more seeds of discontent and the energy he has to put out to keep the accumulated feelings under control must continually be increased. He becomes ever more divided, ever more removed from his real experience and the amount of energy at his disposal for achieving his real life tasks becomes smaller and smaller. This goes on until a situation of stalemate is reached, which takes up all his energy. Then comes the breakdown.

An extreme situation occurs in a partnership, when two people meet again, who have pursued each other in a former life and are old enemies. The result here is a strange mixture of attraction and repulsion. The attraction is based on subconsciously recognising each other and the repulsion on having a foreboding of unresolved tensions. If the attraction is strong enough to result in a partnership, then within a short time a love/hate relationship will develop, accompanied by the most violent emotions. These people will oppose each other most violently and yet they cannot get away from each other. They will continually blame each other with accusations which do not originate in the present, but are memories of earlier mutual malice.

In one case from my practice, a divorced man in about his middle forties had the experience in his regression of being a priest in the Middle Ages. There he had an illegitimate intimate relationship with a village girl, who as a result became pregnant. This fact was annoying for the priest and he had the girl accused of unchastity. As a result of his accusation, she was burnt at the stake, without it ever coming out that he was the one who had seduced her.

In his present life this girl had become his wife and the unconscious memory caused her to make an outburst every time her husband was unreliable, coming home late or not keeping some promise. She countered this unreliability with unrestrained anger and deep-seated hatred and taunted her husband with the most terrible insults. The husband felt somewhat helpless when confronted with this situation and tried to pacify his wife, but he did not succeed. His wife was unconsciously reacting to his former treachery and these deep-seated conflicts finally broke up their marriage. Reconciliation had simply not been possible.

It is a well known fact that love and hatred are very close together. Many present-day partnerships are former enmities and in their present arguments, both sides are trying to solve the old problem. The bondage of one partner is based on his own guilt towards his partner. As a result of his bad conscience, he cannot get away from this person and unconsciously believes that he deserves his state of dependence and that, by enduring the difficult situation, he is paying off an old debt. There are also some avoidance mechanisms so strongly marked that many people only seek out partners who have nothing whatever to do with their own problems. Thus a man who is authoritatively inclined, who cannot stand any contradiction, may exclusively choose partners who submit to him. Or a very jealous man with little self-confidence will seek out a completely unlikely, unattractive partner for life, who will give him no cause for jealousy and therefore not remind him of his sore point. This 'love' is based on the avoidance of problems and of confirmation of what one would like to be. One can like only those people who do not remind one of one's weaknesses. In this way, a problem can sometimes be avoided for a whole lifetime, but it will have to be confronted in a later life. If the avoidance mechanism for once does not work and the above-mentioned jealous man does after all fall in love with a woman, who is not willing to show consideration for his jealousy, the result will be emotional chaos, because without his avoidance mechanism the man feels insecure, he is no longer able to extricate himself from his feelings and feels helpless and defenceless. This meeting can become the most intensively emotional and, subjectively for the man, the unhappiest meeting of his life, if he does not succeed in investigating and discovering the background to his feelings and his behaviour.

We seek in our partner our own former identity. If in a former life we were very energetic and extrovert, but through negative use of these energies, we have blocked out these qualities in our present life and have rather become retiring and inhibited, we now admire the active, outgoing person because he represents a part of our own personality which has now been shut off. We seek a partner with the qualities which we once possessed ourselves in order to reach ourselves again. To put it simply, we look for the ego in the 'thou' in order to win back those parts of ourselves which are lost or else to work through negative parts in this way. It is, however, possible to work through them properly only if one can recognise and put in order the parts concerned in oneself. In that case the significance of the partnership would be changed and would be much more likely to lead to a sensitive restoration if one no longer wrongly projected one's own parts into the 'thou', but rather dealt with them on one's own responsibility.

Each one of us can ask himself: 'How do I stand in relation to myself – How do I judge my own feelings, thoughts and actions? How do I assess them?' That is essential for one's own life. What we do and what we often have the feeling of not being able to do, determine the way we stand in relation to ourselves. These feelings which one has about oneself, are subject to extraordinary distortions, which have their roots in a former life and are the cause of much unnecessary suffering. The man who feels himself stupid and weak, and the girl who feels herself clumsy and ugly, are seldom as stupid and weak, clumsy and ugly as they feel themselves to be. In most cases these feelings are the continuation of feelings in a former life. In psychiatry it has long been known that the feeling which one has about oneself, is a basic and decisive aspect of one's personality.

Serious efforts have been made to discover which influences and experiences take effect on a person's self-confidence. Freud's clinical studies of adults produced his theories about oral and anal libidinous fixations, which shocked and disturbed people so much a generation ago. Today we know that other factors must also play a part. My own experience and also that of many reincarnation therapists long ago led to the conclusion that we bring with us into this world much more than we seem to imagine. We can all look back to painful memories of our childhood. Many of us were forced to eat things we did not like and, as adults, we avoid them. Perhaps now we are adults we stay up too long because in our childhood we were sent to bed too early and we could not bear it. Our behaviour need not necessarily be traced back to former lives.

However, when our parents, our brothers and sisters and other people hurt us by their behaviour, our reactions to this may come from a former life. Being scolded or beaten, having things denied or taken away from us, has perhaps given us the feeling of being unacceptable, inadequate and isolated. But such feelings can just as well derive from a former life.

In our feelings we grow like the skins of an onion. Each day becomes a part of us, just as every day of the past, every day of a former life is a part of us. The struggles and longings of our childhood will remain a part of us, just like the struggles and longings which we bring with us from the past. It takes a long time to accustom ourselves to the idea that old feelings and struggles are not 'over and done with' and that the kernel of our previous lives still exists in us and exercises its influence on us.

Many people will never accept these facts emotionally. We

try to suppress or destroy this part of ourselves. It is not welcome to us in that it does not confirm the picture which we have of ourselves at the present time. I know from personal experience that some people become very uneasy at the idea that they have have Karma from the past to discharge in the present. These are often the very people who have carried on a violent and painful struggle to rid themselves of what was 'foreign' to them and who, in their efforts to face the present are rather punishing and denying themselves.

No one can expect to know everything about his present life, just as, and this is much more understandable, he cannot know everything which once was. However, he can learn to 'remember himself'.

If we become embittered and turn against ourselves, we are split and helpless, incapable of living. Inward bitterness disrupts our life and it should be our task to find a clue to this inward bitterness, this inward pain.

We keep pushing our 'old feelings' further and further down, but this makes it all the more urgent for them to be expressed. Mutual respect is the principle for couples, which can help them to live in harmony with themselves. All our feelings must be properly considered and taken into account. It is a kind of disrespect for ourselves, if we hide, deny or belittle the feeling we have; quite automatically it brings discord within ourselves and creates conflicts – or rather renews conflicts – between our experiences in previous lives and ourselves in the role we are now playing. When we enter into a partnership today, when we get married, then we should know that in that case everyone brings with them their experiences, their identities and their expectations from their previous lives. This is what makes the situation so complicated.

In marriage it is not only the present person, but also the one from the past, who is expressing his or her needs, desires, views, behaviour and longings.

We embark on a partnership in the expectation of meeting old familiar feelings of 'being at home'. But which 'home?' The one of our youth? The one in the last life or the one in a much earlier life? The situation is difficult and for this reason there are often serious conflicts in marriage about unimportant things. All these conflicts, the suppressed feelings, everything which has not been lived to the end, can lead to somatic difficulties and pains, with which a person will be afflicted. Pain is nothing more than feelings misplaced in the body, which can lead to endless suffering. But it is not necessary for this suffering to exist or to continue.

The following ranges of problems are treated during regression:

1. Chronic illnesses and problems

Everything which repeats itself in the body is trying to tell us something, is trying to challenge us to come to terms with something and to learn from it.

This central theme usually goes right back to a former life. The learning process is considerably shortened by reliving the original situation.

2. Emotional over-reactions, eg hopelessness, despair, dejection, rage, aggression

If these emotions occur today from non-traumatic or relatively trifling causes, we may assume that they are the result of former really traumatic and tragic experiences. By experiencing them anew and learning towards what these violent reactions were really directed, we can make the over-reaction superfluous or at least one of only relative importance.

3. Difficulties with certain people or groups of people, such as a parent or the parental home, one's own children, partners, certain types of people

In exactly the same way as unsolved problems must always confront us again, certain people or types of people, with whom an unresolved relationship exists, will also confront us again. In near relations, friends, colleagues and partners, we are often confronted again by people with whom we had difficulties in former lives on account of wrong behaviour on both sides. Encountering them again gives us an opportunity of putting this right.

4. Questions about the meaning of life

Questions about the meaning of one's own life and the tasks which it sets are not at all easy to answer. Basically, everything which presents a problem in a person's life is at the same time a challenge to him and places on him the task of overcoming and solving it. However, since in former lives we often failed in our duty and our responsibility towards our aims, this circumstance brings with it in addition an uncertainty about the present target to be set. Old mistakes made in our endeavours should at all costs be avoided and so it becomes difficult to set oneself any target at all. Here, too, RT can help to make people aware of their past mistakes in setting tasks and formulating aims so that they learn from them.

In order to understand how RT works, it is necessary to consider how the subconscious functions. If ever a life situation becomes too painful or too threatening for anyone, his consciousness switches off partially or completely and the subconscious takes over control. Everything which is perceived during this period of time is unconditionally recorded by the subconscious as if by a tape recorder. Later, when a similar circumstance, a similar perception or a similar feeling comes up, the suppressed event is activated and its original power can be felt, without the actual content of the occurrence being visible. Only the thoughts, the emotions, possibly also the pain become conscious, without the person realising that these come from a former situation.

Whatever was forced down into the subconscious tries to be reintegrated in the consciousness and forces itself up into consciousness in the form of partial experiences, until this aim is realised. This circumstance explains the problems of repetition. The subconscious is timeless, whatever has once been stored in it can at any time be reactivated, no matter how long ago this happened. This confusion of time and place sometimes makes our reaction inflexible and constrained. Therefore it is the task of RT to make what was forced into the subconscious conscious again and thereby to render it harmless.

Every person needs a healthy centre, but he can only find this when he has solved detrimental problems. If problems are not solved in one life, the soul takes these problems with it into the other world. At death the soul leaves the body, but takes with it all its memories, thoughts and deeds, everything which is stored in the subconscious. According to my experience and that of other reincarnation therapists, the soul waits on the other side for a new life in which it will have the opportunity of clearing up those things which it has determined to clear up. Everything which is unfinished at the hour of death is a burden on the soul, which feels the urge to clear up these things in a later life in order thereby to relieve itself of that burden.

Life itself, an understanding of life and a correct way of life are the real prerequisites for learning how to die properly and for the possibility of determining the path of fate beyond death. This is the task which the Egyptian, Tibetan and Islamic books of the dead seek to solve.

In therapy we do not have to handle all the traumas which a person has ever experienced, but rather we have to identify the unbroken thread running through the client's life and find the key experience which inaugurated the chain of events.

With this therapy it takes three months to work through what takes years in psychotherapy, if indeed the latter ever does reach its target, and the result is liberation. The problems disappear. I expect a hundred per cent alteration in the problem. I do not expect the patient to adapt himself to it, to live with it, or say, 'the problem is still there but it does not worry me.' It must simply disappear.

The doctrine of reincarnation is very old, but RT is new.

Everything comes when a person is ready for it and not sooner. The Piscean age was not favourable for people's happiness, it brought us wars, famine, plagues, murders; quite certainly this time was not favourable for reincarnation therapy, but all this has changed in the age of Aquarius. In 1935 an opinion poll asked how many people believed in extrasensory perception, reincarnation and esoteric laws. 95 per cent did not believe in them, 3 per cent were uncertain, 2 per cent believed. In 1979 the same opinion poll was carried out again and the result this time was the other way round. During the years I have been working with reincarnation therapy, I have never been attacked, laughed at or opposed. There have been people who said they did not believe in it, but many people said: 'I do not believe in reincarnation because I do not want to come back and go through the whole thing again.' In reality they meant: 'I do believe in it, but I do not want to think about it. The results are too far-reaching for me.' Most of the people who come to reincarnation therapy are at the stage where they realise that it is they themselves who can do something to solve their problems.

8.

Subjects and Ranges of Problems in RT

The range of subjects in RT is in the main the same as in other psychological therapies: 1. Recurring problems in interpersonal relationships, especially problems connected with the parental home, with partnerships and with certain bodies of people, eg authorities. 2. Fears and over-reactions. 3. Physical afflictions. 4. Questions about the meaning of life.

Problems with the parental home

Even when they have grown up, many people cannot satisfactorily solve and put behind them problems concerned with their own parental home. A person is unable to forgive the parent in question for some behaviour and occupies himself intensively with the question of how far that parent is responsible for his present problems. If the relationship with a parent is particularly tense, accompanied by violent negative emotions, then this parent/child relationship bears the burden of a former life, in which these two people met before and presented each other with serious problems; or else the present parent figure is the mirror image of someone experienced in a very negative way in a former life or it reminds one of a traumatic experience.

Here is an example: A young woman had felt from childhood that her mother was very much prejudiced against her. Her brother got everything and she got nothing. At the present time she feels very restricted, she cannot make full use of her talents and abilities and puts the blame for her present problems on her childhood. In regression it was discovered that the two of them had been together once in a former life as mother and daughter; the daughter had had to look after her crippled mother and was, therefore, very restricted in her private life.

There was a state of mutual hatred between them, which manifested itself in continual quarrelling. One day the daughter took her mother for a walk in a wheelchair and at a lonely spot she pushed her down a steep slope, thereby causing her mother's death. No one saw the accident and the daughter went unpunished.

In another life, again in the same roles of mother and daughter, the mother was a primitive, deranged woman who did not take care of her child and let her starve when she was a baby. The child saw her mother as a witch because she wore long skirts and looked very unkempt and neglected.

In yet another life, the two of them were male rivals fighting for a woman. During the fight the client, in her role as a man, had put out her opponent's eyes and mutilated his body, thereby making him unfit for life.

There were actually more encounters between the two of them, but these three were the most important ones for resolving this woman's present conflicts. She understood now why her mother was prejudiced against her. Unconsciously mother and daughter were reacting to their common experiences in the past. The mother was not in a position to give affection to her daughter, since she still saw her as a hated adversary, a murdress and a neglected child, and this in its turn gave her feelings of guilt. The daughter also had feelings of guilt towards her mother and for this reason had been very susceptible to rejection by her. After this event had been worked through, a normal, objective relationship developed between the two of them, since mutual hatred and reproach had vanished.

In the case of such a strained relationship between two people, if one of them works off his tension, that is sufficient to normalise the relationship. Even if the other one knows nothing about the former life, his subconscious will still react to the new, relaxed attitude of his opposite number and will also relax. Basically, both sides were living out in the present their past situations with all their tensions. Since tensions are not applicable in the present situation, many relationships between people are inexplicable in their peculiarity; reason is here not in a position to solve the problem.

Conflicts with authority

Many people in the presence of those in authority, such as superiors, police, judges, officials, feel themselves restricted and uncertain on the one hand and aggressive on the other.

The subconscious is here remembering earlier times in which human rights were not based on law, and individual authorities had considerably more power over the individual than is the case today. In many cases a person was subjected helplessly to injustice, oppression, torture and humiliation. Oppression was massively present in slavery, the slaves being beaten and punished by being deprived of food and water and being worked to death. Either they died of exhaustion and undernourishment or they dared to rebel and were then tortured to death.

Similar to the life of a slave was that of the serf of a feudal lord, which was all work and hardship. The serfs suffered oppression under the despotism of their lords, they received no wages, their family life was very restricted and also subject to the lord's will.

Today's listlessness, passivity, inability to organise oneself, depression and also aggression may have originated in such oppressive situations. Even the law itself and the moral code often led to oppression. You only have to think of the Middle Ages, in which countless numbers of innocent people were executed, just because they had a liking for medicinal herbs or had entered into an intimate relationship. In such lives it is not only the agonizing death by burning, blood-letting, torture or starvation which is traumatic, but also the invalidation of one's own belief, of one's own convictions, as well as humiliation and exposure, often in public, and the damage to one's human dignity. Present uncertainty, fear of crowds, not wanting to attract attention and feeling uneasy when people look at one, all often go back to events in the Middle Ages, when before a person was executed, the crowds looked at him in anger or scorn and abused him.

Extremely strict tribal rules, which may go right back to tribal life in the Stone Age, contained misanthropic elements. Thus marital infidelity, treachery or lying were punished with death or banishment to a place unfavourable to survival.

Uncertainty and fear of punishment at the present time may still be after effects of this. Last, but not least, are wars, with such occurrences as plunder, rape, murder and loss or separation from one's family. These have left behind them a permanent negative impression. Here, too, authorities have been represented either anonymously, perhaps by an enemy country, or concretely by individual soldiers, or their leader.

Every person has many experiences of oppression stored away in his subconscious and is, therefore, particularly susceptible to certain elements in oppressive situations. Thus someone may be afraid if anyone shouts at him because in a previous life he was killed by a shouting, plundering horde. Someone else may feel unsure of himself in the presence of an authoritative superior, because in a previous life he was whipped to death by an authoritarian foreman. A woman may be afraid of men in uniform, because she was formerly raped and killed by a uniformed soldier. All these susceptibilities go back to an earlier situation when something terrible happened. It is only when the old situations of oppression have been relived and thus neutralised that the fears and over-reactions can disappear, since they are now no longer necessary.

Fears

Specific dread of a particular situation can happen only if there has been a prior experience of it. If we had never had experiences in former lives, we would not know what fear is. Of course, traumatic experiences in this life, such as war experiences, being in danger of one's life or shock also form a basis for fear. All the same, most people's fears are groundless, they have no traumatic cause in this life to explain them. Fears of war and catastrophes often have as a background wars and catastrophes which really were experienced in former lives. Some children are already afraid of war before they have been told very much at all about it. Since everyone has died in a painful way in wars and catastrophes or has lost his loved ones, his house or his livelihood, his subconscious will naturally see war or a catastrophe as something very threatening and will send out to that person a signal of fear.

Fear of vermin and certain kinds of creatures, such as spiders or mice, may go back to the Middle Ages when rats and mice carried the plague. Where there were rats and mice, death and sickness were not far away. In primitive times there were giant insects, which were the natural enemies of man. Thus, for example, giant spiders used to crush a man, spin a web round him and kill him, or giant flying beetles would pounce on a man, break his limbs and eat him up. Whenever there is fear of a specific creature, you can assume that this person met his death in a former life through this creature.

Many people have a fear of heights or depths, of water, of

crowds, of wide or confined spaces and being shut up. These elements may very well have been connected with death in a previous life; someone may have fallen from a tower, suffered shipwreck and been drowned, been pilloried in front of a crowd and then executed, lost his way in an open space, suffocated in a narrow space or starved to death in a prison cell, so that the present fear is pointing to a former death, which the reincarnation therapist must work through, otherwise the fear will go on into the future.

All fears connected with situations can be resolved by regression to the actual fear situation, then working through it thoroughly. Fear is the residue of a situation which has not been inwardly digested. As soon as the experience has been classified and neutralised, the subconscious no longer needs to carry the fear over into the present, since the original trauma is no longer lodged in the subconscious and is no longer falsifying the present. The subconscious must learn that it is not always doing consciousness a service with its warning 'fear!' which proved useful during instinctive development. The case is different with a general fear of death or a phobia. A phobia is always covering up a feeling of guilt or a failure. People punish themselves for some wrong they have done, in this life or a former one, by withdrawing from life and seeing the world around as terrifying. In reality such a person is afraid that the world around might take its revenge on him or find out something unpleasant about him and despise him on that account.

Markedly fearful and modest people are regressed in reincarnation therapy mainly to their aggressive actions and not to anxiety situations, since the latter would only reinforce their present fear. A former tyrant and egocentric punishes himself in a later life by going to the other extreme and becoming helpless and timid with a permanently bad conscience, so that he cannot get on with others. If these people work through their former guilt and aggression, taking responsibility for them instead of suppressing them, they will be able to give up this self-punishment mechanism.

It is the same thing with compulsions – the person in question has not recovered from a shock or he is punishing himself and thwarting his own life because of old feelings of guilt. People with compulsive attitudes are always very hard on themselves, very unkind, they cannot accept themselves as they are and always punish themselves for this with compulsive behaviour. These people direct their negative, destructive intentions more often against themselves than against others. They will not admit to their real desires and needs, nor to their faults. They will not allow themselves any pleasure, but do and think only what brings them problems and makes them depressed. Furthermore they fail to do away with things which cause them problems in life. The subconscious will then seek an outlet for this suppression in compulsion – it is a symbol of what that person is doing psychically: withholding himself from life, going round in a circle in his mind and repressing himself.

Take the case of a young man, who ever since his meeting with a certain girl had been under the compulsion of continu- ally having to wash objects around this girl and after that having to wash his own body. The real cause of this behaviour was to be found in his previous life. In this previous life he had worked as a servant to a very strict, bad-tempered mistress who once, as a punishment for some fault, had him tarred and feathered and put on show. This treatment was exceedingly painful. The hot tar burnt his skin; washing away the tar equally caused pain and burning. Afterwards his skin burnt and itched and in pain and anger he ran about like an animal. In addition he suffered being put on show and the shame of people laughing at him. As soon as this event was discovered, the compulsion to wash himself stopped immediately, although it was very strongly marked before regression. The present girl, in her nature, reminded this young man of his former mistress and his subconscious reacted by reproducing the physical symptoms like a gramophone record. This is a typical example of the subconscious mixing up time and space. Just because someone with a similar nature had appeared in the present surroundings, it replayed the whole occurrence in its physical effect.

Over-reactions are exaggerated ways of behaving in which someone may live with uncontrolled rage, be overtaken by panic or be overcome by boundless sorrow. An exaggerated sexual drive is an over-reaction and there are many more. In the view of present psychotherapy, over-reactivity is a diversion tactic, an unconscious avoidance of conflict. In RT one investi- gates the reason for this over-reaction and assumes that this behaviour comes from a previous experience. If, in a previous life, someone was, through lies and treachery, cheated of an inheritance or a position which was due to him, the slightest untruth may throw him into a rage. Some therapies practised today provoke over-reactions in order to make them die away. Such designs do not get to the heart of the matter. You can keep on provoking someone to anger without him finding out the origin of his anger. A therapy will be effective only when the primary cause of such behaviour is discovered and the underlying emotions have also been laid bare. Thus below the anger there is usually failure, below the failure there is fear, below the fear there is cowardice and weakness. Working on the upper layer of emotion alone leaves the layers below it untouched.

Physical afflictions, like over-reactions, often have their cause in previous lives. A dull pain in the region of the heart may result from having been buried alive. The person in question may have been squashed up against a wall or he may have been trampled underfoot. A young woman kept on having trouble with her left foot; first it was sprained, then squashed and injured in sport. The cause turned out to be that, in a former life when fleeing from some soldiers, she had in her haste stepped into a hole and heavy stones had squashed her foot. She could not get out and her flight had been in vain.

The question about the purpose of life is of course a basic one, which a person asks himself during the course of his development; but this question often arises in situations where a person is frustrated in his life. After too much pain and loss, there is often nothing left but the question 'What is it all for?' or 'Why me?' In the question about the meaning of life, our own former opinions also stand in our way. In the case of a young man who, whenever anything happened to him kept asking if this was God's will, we found out that in a former life he had been a priest and had imposed rigid rules on those in his charge, put them in fear of God's punishment; he had not stopped short of torturing them for their sins. During the torture he told the victims that it was God's will and that it was taking place in God's name. This arbitrary statement of God's purpose led to similar thoughts going round and round in his head today.

The development of a human being

A soul incarnating on the earth today usually already has hundreds or thousands of lives on earth behind it. During these many lives the soul tries to overcome its difficulties and to complete certain learning processes. In doing so, it finds itself in very similar circumstances in many lives and repeatedly encounters the same problems. If a person oppressed others in former lives, he will find himself in conditions of oppression until he recognises that what he does to others applies equally to himself. If someone has done something to others, he must suffer the same thing himself, until he has learnt not to make any difference in value and respect between himself and others. It is necessary to recognise that all creatures are of the same substance and have the same potential and to learn to treat one's own life and that of others in a responsible manner. If someone has earlier refused responsibility, the original desire not to take any responsibility will be strengthened by his being born into life situations in which he will be given absolutely no responsibility, eg into oppressed, disadvantaged classes of society.

On the other hand one may also be burdened by fate with so much responsibility that it is impossible to discharge it properly and one will be bound to make mistakes. Both these manifestations are only processes for learning how to behave rightly in respect of responsibility at the right moment, ie how to accept it. If someone shirked an important decision in a former life, because he was too cowardly to accept the consequences, he may in later lives be treated as immature by the world around him and he may even be denied the right to make decisions at all or he may be faced with such difficult decisions that it is impossible for him to make the right choice. In my experience, one needs a whole lot of lives in order to make up for a mistake one has made.

The goal is to master the challenge at every stage of development. The soul must be able to feel calm and at ease in all situations and difficulties. If it builds up resistance to something, it must demolish this again during its process of development, through being confronted again and again with the same situations until it can remain neutral in its attitude even to things which are disagreeable to it. A too strongly marked ego and a superiority complex can lead to resistance to fate, since one's own will does not agree with what occurs. The old-fashioned word 'humility' takes on a new meaning when one's own will is broken by fate, and the soul learns also to accept things which do not please it.

The fundamental mistake which a soul can make is not to accept responsibility for its own actions. This involves self-deception and betrayal of one's own conscience. Since self-deception represents a voluntary limitation of consciousness and perception, this wish becomes strengthened and the soul becomes less conscious and less capable of perception. It then suffers under these circumstances and tries to release itself from them again. However, this can happen only if it becomes aware again of the original self-deception. This happens in a cycle of several lives.

When once the soul arrives on the earthly plane, it will incarnate on this planet only until it has mastered the tasks for which it was sent here. Most people have been incarnating on the earth from very early times. Before the human form, there also exist memories of incarnations in animals and plants, right back to single-celled forms of life. Experiences from non-human incarnations often come up during regression and these also contain traumatic material. In the animal kingdom traumas are represented by occurrences of being eaten or wounded or dying of starvation; in the vegetable kingdom of being dried up by barren weather conditions, being torn up or damaged or being trodden underfoot by men or animals.

Before the earth, the soul has past memories of life on other planets, which can look very different. On many planets, technology was and is far in advance of the earth, and memories emerge of inter-stellar space travel, of robot-like bodies, of forms of society guided by computers with firm control of the life of the individual. On yet other planets there are bodies similar to man, many of them considerably larger or smaller than ours, but similarly constructed. Depending on the level of consciousness, the forms of society were either very much standardised with very strict rules and moral codes or else free in thought and action.

9.

Reincarnation and Spirit

Karma and reincarnation: two concepts which give human life an inner meaning; two concepts which the East has, but which the West, at the Councils of Nicea, Trent and Constantinople, removed from its religion. Karma and reincarnation mean taking on a form at certain frequencies, as for example, on the physical plane; being born in order to act out certain kinds of connections and situations; putting an end to certain adherences by overcoming them; and re-establishing the inner freedom of the soul. In its free state the soul fixes no aims and has no desires, it is one with the One. From the Zen-Buddhist point of view, as soon as we are in the one, there is no longer any One. We can perceive the one only when we are two. Perhaps the reason why the soul left the plane of the One was in order to be able to perceive the One from the other viewpoint. Here duality arose.

If we set out with the assumption that the soul has required and then willed of its own accord all the experiences it has had, then our daily life and the suffering of humanity take on a completely different meaning. We recognise ourselves as beings who have proceeded into the physical plane in order to carry out certain perceptual processes and each experience in our daily life is a part of this process. From the Karmic point of view, every life is a new opportunity to extend the scope of our experience, to develop our potential, to recognise that we and we alone fix the cause of our experience.

The acceptance of this responsibility brings knowledge and freedom; the negation of it brings ignorance and lack of freedom, if one continually seeks the causes from the outside instead of the inside. We do not find the sense of life in the philosophy of materialism. It is not the case that we are identical with our bodies and that when life is over, all is over, so let us take what we can now since there is nothing after death. On the basis of more conscious experience, philosophical materialism no longer appears valid. From a more conscious level, we can say that in consequence of birth into our present life, we have taken on a certain task and are trying to carry it out. In the reincarnation sense, it simply does not enter into the question whether our bodies and our souls are in connection with hereditary factors from our parents or whether our personality is influenced by absorbing standards of value through education and contact with society. We do not know how many hereditary factors are handed down through our genes. The soul has the possibility of seeking out from these hereditary factors what it needs for its development and the task it has set itself.

Education and society provide a person with certain situations, but what he makes of them is his affair and his alone. No one can refer to outside circumstances as the cause of his behaviour; rather, the outside circumstances are just stimuli which bring out the inner factors. A person knows from his birth exactly what he is thereby letting himself in for. We say to ourselves: I will choose these parents, this experience. This is the life I shall have, perhaps with only one eye or sitting in a wheelchair. I shall be killed in a car accident. That is exactly the experience I need in order to make progress. The experiences are not programmed in advance in every detail and the person has a whole palette of possibilities in dealing with his coming life and influencing it: but the aim and the theme of his life are fixed before birth. In the sense of reincarnation, the whole physical plane is just a school of development. When we learn that everything existing on this earth is necessary schooling for the person now incarnating on it, we shall cease to complain of injustice and misery; instead we shall consider the earth as a stage on which all kinds of problems can be handled and all joys and pleasures can be experienced. Help takes on quite a different meaning – help does not mean helping someone to avoid troubles or sympathising with him, but rather helping him to understand his fate, to accept it and to alter it. We no longer make a value judgment, we no longer condemn. Everyone receives and brings about the very experience which he needs.

In the view of the tarot, the moon is the symbol of self-discovery and in the doctrine of archetypes, according to C.G.

Jung, the moon is the eternal feminine, which is subject to the soul.

In the individual phases of the moon, the heavenly body of the night shows itself to be subject to the laws of death and rebirth. Simple people believe they can recognise the changeless rhythm of their own lives in the moon cycle. In very early times people discovered its influence on ebb and flow; but it also came to be connected with illness and death and with fertility and resurrection. In a Babylonian hymn, the moon was celebrated as the womb, which gives birth to everything; the Greek Silene (the moon) was at the same time goddess of growth and of birth. The Egyptian moon god, Thoth, was looked on as Lord of Time and Reckoner of the Years. The moon played an important role in the magical and picturesque religious symbolism of most peoples. This depended on the fact that its form is constantly changing, that it is obviously connected with various life rhythms on earth and that it became an important point of reference for reckoning time. The moon is closely connected with fertility and so with everything which is born and dies. The moon existed in our former incarnations and will exist in our coming lives.

Through discovery of ourselves in former lives, we again admit parts of ourselves which have been suppressed or unkindly treated. This corresponds to the moon principle. For once to become conscious of the whole content of our souls, to descend to the deepest levels, to reintegrate parts which have become separated, that is the principle of RT. We do not need to *do* anything for our development, first of all we must find out who we *are*.

Every living being, every object we meet is an indication, a lesson which has come to us. We often do not recognise this because of our egocentric inclinations and desires. Possessive desires make us dependent. Freedom is meeting oneself. As long as this meeting does not take place, we cannot be happy without desire and we project this desire of meeting ourselves on to innumerable other desires.

However wishes are thoughts. Wishes reveal themselves by means of thoughts. As we know, thoughts are charged with energy. For this reason thoughts can possess a dynamic of their own and can develop further.

Before every deed, there was a thought. The real purpose is

not always apparent, especially when a calculating purpose lies behind the deed.

The following kinds of thoughts possess particularly high charges of energy: beliefs; intentions, decisions; justifications; calculations; wishful thinking.

An attitude towards a person or thing is a value judgment made by the person adopting the attitude. Since such judgments can never be complete and objective, they represent only a part of the total value of the person or thing concerned. Calmness – without judgment – is probably the highest condition of the soul. It can tolerate everything and let everything exist, because everything has a right to its own being. As soon as the soul begins to make judgments, it will adopt certain attitudes and will thereby become subjective and limited. The attitude which one adopts creates the reality. If someone's attitude is 'you have to work hard in order to achieve your aim' or 'you don't get anything handed to you on a plate', then this attitude is typical of himself and of others whom he attracts, because they have similar points of view. Every thought is a soul's creation; it makes itself independent and, according to its content, attracts corresponding situations and feelings to itself. One can observe this particularly easily in the law of Karma. Someone thinks: 'You can safely oppress these people', or 'they are not worth being treated any better' and in that same life or a later one this person will come across others, who have the same opinion of him and think 'he could safely be oppressed, he is not worth anything'.

Firm convictions originate in the movement of polarity. A person has recognised in one of his lives that he has paid too little attention to his own needs and has not valued himself sufficiently highly. Now, after his death, he makes the resolution: 'I must do more for myself' and in his next life he assiduously looks after his own needs and lives for them. He can then express such convictions as 'One should not neglect oneself'; he may adopt such principles as 'You can only love others if you love yourself', etc. A man arrives at firm convictions and principles only from the opposite polarity. Someone who has defrauded people in the past, resolves to be honest in his next life. He is then later of the opinion: 'One should not take anything away from anyone', 'I must not tell lies to anyone'. This may go as far as exaggerated conviction or even fanaticism. We 'forget' our old trains of thought and intentions, but all the same they run their course, like a planet with its own individual speed and rhythm. It can take a long time before the effect of the original thought catches up with us. A person who used to think, 'I don't have to worry about other people, I don't need anyone', wonders in a later life why he has no friends and other people do not want to know anything about him. Without noticing what is happening, the world around him is adapting his original attitude and acting in accordance with the way he used to think, although now he positively wants friends. If someone in a partnership used to think, 'I won't let anyone near me any more, I don't want anything more to do with anyone', this person is surprised in a later life if he cannot find a partner. In reality he himself and the world around him are obeying his earlier thoughts, which have not lost their power.

Deep-seated convictions derive from our traumatic experiences. After too much sorrow we say: 'I will never take a risk again', 'Never again will I trust another person'. After a failure, the soul acquires a firm conviction. It has not managed to be calm, tolerant and all-loving and now it sees as the only solution a 'patent solution', ie the firm conviction which one only has to acquire in order to prevent any further difficulties arising. However, a too-sweeping opinion can no longer be objective and spontaneous, and so cannot really resolve the situation either; instead it throws up new problems, since the firm conviction tries to cast in its mould situations to which it is not suited, thus producing conflicts, upsets and problems.

Resolutions, such as 'never again. . .' apply rigidly to both poles of duality. Every 'never again' has the force of a suggestion, the 'never' and 'not' being put in brackets. Everything one 'does not' want, one gets; everything one 'does not' want to see will force itself upon one; everything which ought 'not' to exist, exists particularly strongly in our consciousness. Therefore positive thinking is often not enough to solve real problems with negative content. First one should track down the contents of the original thought and find out in which situation one accepted this thought as a firm conviction. One should discover what the real failure was and find another, more direct method of solving the problem. This also involves a modification of the original thought, changing it into a neutral form. 'Lying is a sin' can become a modified attitude, such as: 'I will endeavour not to lie. When a lie seems to be necessary, I would like to get to the bottom of this apparent necessity and approach the subject in a more open way.' 'You can't trust anyone' can become 'You can't trust everyone. Basically I am trying to trust, but I do not exclude the possibility that other people may have deceitful intentions.'

The 'never again' type of thinking swings us to and fro like a pendulum; for a while we are on the side of dualism; for a while on the other; sometimes both sides are in conflict. In order to solve a problem, one only has to recognise the different components of that problem and establish when and why one created the various aspects of the matter. If, in former lives, one forsook people for egoistical reasons, in other lives, as counter pole, one becomes dependent on them and so, through the diversity of intentions and energies, a problem now arises.

In RT we look into our former lives, where we ourselves have given way to these various forces and have lived through every one of them, until they are no longer in opposition to each other. We cannot avoid assuming responsibility for all aspects of a problem, for there can really be nothing in our way except what we ourselves have placed there.

Alibis and justifications (excuses) also have a tendency to materialise. If a warlord started a war on the pretext that his people had not got enough to eat, but this was not the real reason, which was rather to satisfy his own pugnacity, then in a later life he may find himself in exactly the situation which he had 'created' and brought forward as a pretext. He prepared this reality in advance with his thoughts. He can then later go hungry himself as a citizen or he may at some time really be faced with the problem of a starving population. If someone in the present gives a 'headache' as the excuse not to attend a meeting, although he has not got a headache and just does not want to keep the appointment, then within a short time a real headache may appear. If a son who is to take over his father's business shirks the responsibility of making the decision and puts this off with the excuse that 'he does not feel sure enough yet', then quite soon he may be faced with the problem of uncertainty, perhaps in a completely different connection.

We often use a particular justification for many lives on end. It allows us to keep on making the same mistake because we are putting ourselves in the right. 'After all I've got to live too', a thief may think, when he is robbing his victim and then beating him up, 'he can't do anything with his money anyway'. He does not know that he is here sending out a boomerang, which later on, when he has long since forgotten this kind of justification and has perhaps meanwhile become an upright man, will come back to him, perhaps in the form of being allotted some money, but not being able to do anything with it, not being able to get at it, or perhaps it may even bring him misfortune in the form of money losses (then too he would not be able to do anything with the money). 'After all, I've got to live too' can lead to a situation in which he cannot die and feels himself condemned to live on. 'After all, she doesn't love her husband' a woman may think, when she is having an affair with a married man, 'at least he has a good time with me.' This can later lead to circumstances in which this woman is either not loved at all or only because of some material advantage; or people do not believe in her love. Justifications and calculations are the most complicated trains of thought, since on the surface they appear rational and correct, but in reality they are just camouflage for wrong behaviour and deceit. They are not always easy to discover, because the person concerned has considered them of vital importance and has constructed in his mind a fine edifice in which everything is right and proper, everything has its reason and everything can be explained. A person will often hold on stubbornly to his justifications, because he would otherwise have to admit that he has for a long time been on the wrong track, only he has not yet confessed it.

Wishful thinking has its origins in traumatic events and guilty deeds, as a result of which something negative is pushed far into the background. One does not want to admit to one's own identity and therefore identifies oneself with a more pleasant one. Every emphasis on one's own positive attitudes is already a mild form of wishful thinking, if the intention is thereby to suppress the opposite negative ones. Seeing everything through rose-coloured spectacles and setting impossibly high targets can have an unforeseen opposite effect. Every target for which one strives has its negative opposite pole, from which one wants to get away. After a life spent as a prostitute, a soul may in the next life go into a convent and try to become 'holy'. The problem is immediately solved if one can accept both aspects of one's personality and of the desire and no longer identify only with one side.

The further back in time one goes when regressing, the greater and more rapid is the effect of the power of thought. A soul's thought, such as 'I want to experience something now' will immediately bring it into a situation in which it does 'experience something', only it has not defined the quality of what it wants to experience. People often think: 'It can't go on like this, I can't bear it any longer', but they leave this thought as it is, without converting the first impulse in a constructive way. What happens next? There is a misfortune, an accident, and they have achieved what they wanted: 'it can't go on like this'. Fate has taken them at their word. If they do not recognise the connection, they may become even more unhappy about it. 'I just haven't enough time, something must change' can lead to a broken leg, which makes us go into hospital, where we have plenty of time and also the change we wanted; only we can't do as much with our newly-won time, because we are handicapped. Thoughts too loosely formulated can lead to unpleasant surprises. When once we have understood that fate is just obeying our thoughts, opinions and decisions (even with a time lag of several lives) it becomes easier for us to handle it. One has to accept responsibility also for one's earlier thoughts and intentions, even if one has in the meantime moved away from them. The special dynamic of the old thoughts can cease only when the person has fully integrated them again. In RT, the therapist wants to know the previous attitude, the expectation and purpose of every action, because although the mode of procedure, the tool, may change, the purpose often remains the same for many lives. In the case of guilty actions, the therapist wants to know the justification and the calculation, in order to make his client fully aware of these old thoughts, to take away their hidden power and to prevent them continuing further, like a programme of which we are unconscious, but which forces us to go on making the same mistakes over and over again in order to prove to ourselves that it can not have been so wrong after all. Responsibility does not begin with the deeds but with the thought. Once this has been realised, it should not be difficult to form one's thoughts constructively without continually having to control them.

Man's life is always accompanied by error. What distinguishes human beings from all other species is not so much that they have split the atom, invented radar or gone into space as that they have the capacity to make mistakes. An animal is never mistaken, it knows immediately. The gigantic arsenal of our science is in reality nothing but a device to make up for the lack of a minimum of direct, simple wisdom. We provide ourselves with thousands of arms and antennae, with which we replace direct reactions. In the midst of a giant machine, which we consider all powerful, we ourselves are completely powerless. If the machine fails, we are inferior beings, 'something that is not as harmonious as a tree or flower, not as calm as a stone, not as strong as an animal, something really debased. Truly that is human inferiority' (Sri Aurobindo).

The Law of Karma is always the vital touchstone in tracing the origins of events in a human life. Everything outside as well as inside, what we consider as our ego, is the result of what preceded it – and will itself become the cause of a later effect. With Karma it is a matter of ethics. We achieve bad results when we act badly and good ones when we do good. Actions, words and thoughts are like little seeds, which already carry the conditions for blossom within themselves. From life to life these seeds ripen into plants, whose fruits we harvest. Bad seeds result in bad plants, healthy seeds result in healthy plants and sound fruit.

The reason why we ever do things which lead to bad results is our basic ignorance of the existence of the spirit. Our ignorance is like the darkness of a clouded night sky. Through it our actions are like the attempt in complete darkness to shoot with bow and arrows at an invisible target.

From this total ignorance, this complete unconsciousness, arises our conception of a duality, of an 'I' and of something which we experience as separate from this 'I'. This wrong conception leads to the six distinctive poisons of the spirit: hate, lust, folly, pride, jealousy and covetousness. These lead to the three evil actions of the body, the four evil actions of speech and the three evil actions of the spirit, namely: murder, theft, sexual misconduct; lying, slander, gossip, coarse speech; envy, bad will and distorted views.

Actions resulting from such previous indications are bad, because they lead to sorrow. We should not inflict on others anything which we would not permit to happen to our loved ones or to ourselves. Instead we should carry out actions which are the opposite of the bad ones; saving the life of other beings, being magnaminous in every way, having a positive sex life, telling the truth, only speaking when it is useful, spreading unity, speaking reassuringly, being content, having sympathy with all living creatures, practising a positive way of life in every respect.

We must work with the spirit. If the spirit is evil, the result is coarse speech and aggressive action; if the spirit is good, everything resulting from it will be good. What is inside us, now as well as at death, is the cause of all happiness, but also of all sorrow. Thus we experience various kinds of worlds, according to the mood we are in. One day everything is fine, because we are happy; something good from the past has awakened in us. Another day everything is dark, because we are in a bad mood; in that case the fruit of bad thoughts and deeds has ripened in us. When our spirit leaves the body after death, the same thing occurs, only the differences become much greater. A bird in the air casts scarcely any shadow, but when it lands, the shadow is clearly visible. In the same way, after death our Karma comes to light. Due to a lack of these external sense impressions, the spirit begins to work on what is inside itself. If this is full of good impressions, it experiences these as if on a good day, when everything is fine and the result is a strong feeling of happiness, since we are not held back by the sense impressions of the body. The spirit remains in this state for some time, as long as is necessary to assimilate the realisations of the life which has just been. After that deeper impressions will emerge and determine what the spirit will experience next and what kind of life it will go on to.

10.

Case Histories

The sufi master Jalal-ud Din Rumi (1207–1273) once said: 'If you want to know yourself, then realise that you are made of two things. One is the outer shell, which is called the body, which you can see with your outer eye. The other is that inner part, which is sometimes called the soul, sometimes the spirit and sometimes the heart, and which can be recognised by the inward eye. This inner part is your true being, everything else is just its retinue, its army and its attendants.'

By quoting in this last section some examples of actual cases, we would like to demonstrate how the inner part works. Who better to report on it than those people who have themselves had experience of reincarnation therapy. I would, therefore, like to report these cases and the experience they contain from the point of view of my clients.

Let us first take the report of Joe Z.

'I am nearly 60 years old and have had two careers in picture-book publishing. My first career ended at the age of 28 when my first marriage broke up and my prospects were not good. I had a pile of debts and was at a low ebb. But during my second marriage I achieved what as a young man I had always dreamed about: I was able to work my way up to the top management of my firm, even though I had not had the education that others can show today. I was a careerist, always demanding better and more frantic achievements from myself. I was a high flyer and everyone knew it. What no one knew was that I suffered from inferiority complex, inhibitions, uncertainty and anxiety. I had suppressed all feelings of closeness and warmth, I was unapproachable and as a result had difficulties in my relations with other people. As I grew older, I was troubled by questions about life, which I was less and less able to suppress. All my life, books have been my companions, above all I read the classics, such as Goethe, but also the great masters of philosophy, like Carl Gustav Jung. At some time or other I came across books dealing with reincarnation with former lives, with Karma and so on. This was new territory for me and at first I was sceptical about them. How was I to suspect that it was here that the way to freedom would lie for me. For many years I carried my problems of youth and education around with me. My father died when I was three months old, so for the whole of my youth I had no manly example to copy and no fatherly guidance. I attributed all my problems to the fact that I had grown up without a father. But at some time or other I realised that these explanations were too simplistic.

'When I decided to try reincarnation therapy, I had a perfectly clear aim in view. I wanted at last to become a complete person, to know what were the real causes of my problems. I wanted to know the meaning of this life, and the extent to which fate was responsible. My first visit to Frau Vallieres was marked by varying expectations, but also by anxiety. My scepticism led me to decide not to undergo therapy immediately , but first to attend one of Frau Valliere's seminars. She was soon able to gain my confidence and I have never regretted taking this step.

'Thanks to reincarnation therapy, I was soon able to establish a relationship with my father, and also with my mother, who had died in the meantime. The fact that my relationship with my mother was much more comprehensive and more transparent than I could ever have imagined was, and still remains for me, a very beautiful and profound experience, although during therapy it was not only pleasant things which came to light.

'For me, reincarnation therapy meant hard work. Naturally, soon after the first sessions I wondered whether what I was seeing and experiencing was really a part of my past, or whether my imagination had a part in it. Today, I know that it was all just as I relived it. The therapy was accompanied by anxieties. I experienced my very wrong behaviour in former lives and what was very painful for me was to be obliged to live again through all the sorrows which I had ever experienced and suffered in former lives. That brought anxiety with it. On the other hand, this anxiety was natural to me. With every session of therapy I advanced one step further. Above all, the genuinely penetrating 'interpretational' discussions with my therapist were of the greatest importance. The result was that after each one I worked very hard and intensively on myself. Life became simpler and easier for me. I feel that powers have been released in me, which are developing further. The word 'humility' has acquired a specially personal meaning for me. Where previously there was a sense of power or pride, but also an inward emptiness, I now feel gratitude and humility. That is essentially deeper, better, more beneficial and more lasting than pride and arrogance. Reincarnation therapy has had a very positive effect on my whole life. Today I experience everything much more intensely and more deeply. Today I am 'on the way', as they say – on the way to becoming more of a person in the here and now. I feel myself to be deeper and more spontaneous, I also live out my feelings and my perceptions consciously and affirmatively. I am on the way and have long ago realised: 'There is still a lot to do. All that matters is to be on the way. . .'

Rita R's report of her experiences reads entirely differently. It is more direct and spontaneous and lets us share her experience of what happened. Rita R. came to therapy because she had problems with people in authority. In addition she could not handle her clairvoyant abilities.

'Flood – go back in time (from now, in centuries) BC 3000, 3100, 3200, 3300 starting with 3000 BC, I get a strong reaction, the last dates are weak, it may be an after-effect. A picture appears before me: the Near East centring on Iraq, then I see water, a lot of water, which has flooded the land.

'I am on a very high ziggurat with a broad staircase made of glazed clay tiles. The zigurat has three storeys (pyramid steps, the lowest for the people, the middle for the state and religious ruling class, the top for the king, the priests, etc). On the walls of the staircase, light blue mosaics (precious stones) in patterns of stars.

'I am an astronomer priest. It is night time. I look at the sky which is full of stars. I see a star crossing the path of the others. This star becomes a little larger, it is trailing a tail of light behind it, which is broader and not so bright at the end, (from where I am) it looks about 40 cm broad. This star is getting bigger and bigger, it must be a comet, but it is unknown to me and puzzling. Now it is about 12 cm across, red-gold to brown-gold. Its tail is gold, red, brown, it is rushing along at great speed. I know many comets, but I have never seen one like this. Red-gold and reddish comets are supposed to bring bad luck and ruin. The next day I look at the sky, it is bright blue, shading to deep blue. I look for the comet, but there is nothing to be seen in the sky. I am very thoughtful about the sighting of the comet and I run about in agitation up the ziggurat. The countryside is dry, mountains are to be seen in the distance; peasants are watering their fields and working in them. Down in the town there is a lot of activity in the market and in the harbour. At round about midday the sun becomes more and more yellow and bigger. (I do something wrong or behave wrongly.) I should be able to see the comet because it has reached the earth's orbit, but I don't see it. I am running about up the ziggurat very perplexed and rather agitated, I go into my private niche in the temple in order to pray to my god (there are two gods). The god says to me: "Misfortune will come to the people, water will come, but keep silent". The sun is getting bigger and yellower all the time, now I would say it has reached a diameter of about one metre. The people in the fields and down in the town are observing this too. They are pointing at the sun, saying: "Look here, the sun is so yellow and so big and is getting bigger and yellower all the time, what does it mean?" They are getting worried and excited.

'The king comes to the ziggurat with his retinue. Musicians with wind instruments place themselves on both sides of the staircase and play. The king comes up the stairs with his household. Since I am responsible for the weather, for foretelling events and for fixing dates, the king asks me why I have not drawn his attention to the present event. He wants to throw me into prison. I ask, who then should take my place. I go down on my knees and humbly ask for his forgiveness. I try to explain to him that it is all happening so quickly.

'Whilst I am still having a discussion with the king, a howling storm arrives. A sandstorm, reddish-brown hides the sun. it becomes dark, a very strong wind blows everything away. We go back inside to the wall niches, everything happens terribly quickly. The king gives instructions to his officials that no ships must be allowed to sail on the sea or on the rivers; the peasants must go home from the fields. I go into a large niche in the temple. In the floor there is a round hollow with pitch burning in it. We sit in front of it in a semi-circle, our eyes directed towards a picture of gods on the wall at the back, which contains little pieces of golden mosaic, otherwise the room is blackened by soot. I am sitting in the middle, sprinkling incense and other essences on to the fire. Something is brought up from below as an offering and thrown into the fire in order to make the gods change their mind and avert the misfortune. (It is not a blood sacrifice.) Then come dark clouds which cover everything. It is getting very dark, it is beginning to rain hard, a cloudburst, the sun is no longer to be seen, the sky is reddish-brown to black, I can no longer see any stars in the night. I cannot make any more observations.

'I go up to the king in the ziggurat to show him my charts. I usually observe the stars with the naked eye, but I have a few instruments, something like a model zodiac, and circles, a clay circle in which I inscribe the position of the stars. I see the following picture: the sign pisces very fully occupied by the sun, the moon, Mercury, Venus, Mars, Jupiter and others, Uranus is in Cancer in opposition to Saturn in Capricorn and both of these are square to the sun and moon. Neptune appears to be at the end of Pisces and the comet was also passing through this sign the last time I saw it. There is such a strong, howling storm blowing that we are almost being torn down from the ziggurat and, holding on tightly, we go inside again. Objects are being blown away by the wind. The trees below are bending. The roofs (of straw) are being blown off the houses. The sky is dark and gloomy, reddish-brown or black. Scarcely anything can be seen. It is raining and raining non-stop, the water is beginning to rise and keeps on rising. The people are uneasy, agitated, they are trying to save themselves, first up trees or in boats or on pieces of wood. The water goes on rising and is covering an ever greater area, then some very high waves come from the sea, about six to ten times as high as the huts. They break, roaring onto the land, the boats and ships are wrecked, the people go down screaming, the water is howling, rising, dragging everything along with it. Some officials are coming back to the ziggurat. With them the people are pressing upwards, the town is very large and there certainly isn't room for all of them on this great ziggurat. The people are pressing up the steps. When the water reaches the first section, those below pull down the ones above them. There is wild chaos, everyone wants to save himself. Then the sky is seen to be glowing reddish-brown. Glowing fragments of the comet (like stones) are driving across the sky in a broad band from the west–south–west. (During regression, the name typhon kept coming to me for the comet.) After some weeks of continual rain, the water reaches the middle part of the ziggurat. The king and I and a few others withdraw into the upper rooms of the middle part. Through square holes in the walls we observe the land. The water is rising and rising. It is hopeless. Soon it will reach us too and now it is already coming in under the wooden doors. I push the door open. The water is up to my neck, then it rises higher, swallows us up and with us the whole ziggurat and all the people. The waves howl. There is nothing more to be seen but dark water.'

Klaus H.:

'I first heard of reincarnation therapy (RT) in 1982, but I was very sceptical. Since I had been interested in the field of esoterics for about seventeen years, I was familiar with the idea that consciousness lives through many existences. At the same time I had quite often encountered the sort of remarkable manifestations which one can confidently dismiss as charlatanism. My mistrust was, therefore, considerable. It was not until 1984 that it was changed into interested curiosity, when a friend directed my attention to the serious method of Netherton/ Shiffrin. After studying Dr Netherton's book *A Report on Life before Life*, I decided to give RT a trial. Of course I thought 'It is not really necessary' but I hoped through the therapy to obtain some 'proof' of reincarnation.

'This notion was put out of my head by Frau Vallieres during the very first phone call. Since hope of this kind was not the only – or indeed the most important – reason for my interest in RT, I went to Frau Vallieres for treatment at the end of 1984.

'There I got to know about thirty of my former lives, which all have an influence – sometimes a very subtle one – on my present life. From the wealth of impressions, episodes and scenes, I can of course pick out only a few.

'For a large part of the population of Europe, the problem of authority is at the present time one of the decisive factors. In my case, this is clearly apparent from what seem to be my last two lives, which took place very probably in Germany or France (Alsace Lorraine the life before last) and in France or possibly in England (my last life) between 1914 and 1934. First there appears in a playground a girl of about 5 or 6 years, delicately built with long fair hair. She does not feel happy, because this playground is being guarded by men in uniform, who frighten her. These guards have to leave the playground very quickly because 'a raid' is coming; so it must be wartime (1st World War). At some time when one of these raids comes, I decide defiantly not to obey instructions (to go into the cellar), but I remain outside in our little street. I am feeling happy: "Now I'll show them, nothing will happen to me!" Then there's a terrific noise, an enormous tank comes round the corner and I'm frightened to death. I'm almost paralysed and stand rooted to the spot. The tank comes straight at me, runs me over and my body is squashed.

'It is easy to learn the main lesson from this life, because the same pattern is repeated in many other lives. I have always rebelled against any kind of authority, without making any distinction between when it is sensible to do so and when it is not. In this case, disregard of well-founded authority led to immediate death. This experience became built into my consciousness but so too did examples of tyrannical authority with which I have had more than my share of involvement. During RT, what was probably my last life appeared immediately after the death of the little girl, with scarcely any transition period. In this connection I should explain that, probably because of the suddenness of this death, it had scarcely registered on my consciousness. Similarly my reincarnation followed immediately, this time again into a female body. The first scene (which leads to my death) shows me aged about 18 or 19, with my husband. We are quarrelling. He hits me and swears at me, calling me a whore and a slut. I am pregnant, but not by him. During the argument I am enraged and throw my unfaithfulness in his face (thinking as I do so: "At last I've shown him and got him where it hurts"). Finally he chases me out of the house and I run away, somewhat hurt and shaken, because I hadn't really expected that of him. As though numbed, I run through the busy streets totally lost in thought. I come to a square; completely absentmindedly I climb over the railing, taking no notice of the roaring traffic and as a consequence I am hit by a car. My body strikes the road hard, the right side of my head is cut open, blood pours out. In the hospital I lose my baby, I have lost too much blood and I die.

'How did I come to hate and despise my husband? By marring this man, who was at least 10 years older than I was, I hoped to get away from the parental home and to be free from force situations. However, right from the beginning, I realised that I did not love him. My husband already knew that before we were married because I told him, but he believed that he would be able to make me love him and to 'train' me in other ways as well. There he was barking up the wrong tree! When I realised that I had jumped out of the frying pan into the fire, there were continual scenes, not only because he kept on making up my mind for me, but also because he was often away for weeks on end (he was a commercial traveller or something of that sort). I got the petting I craved from other men, which soon led to my becoming pregnant and finally to the event I have just described.

'A result of this life was that I decided I would become a man in the next life, so that I could at last be 'free'. Certainly I am male in this life, but what a disappointment: I am living in a world in which women are becoming increasingly emancipated; so I've missed the mark! Although outwardly the two lives appear so different, their structure is the same. It is a pair of opposites: authority (which I equated with force situations) and self-assertion (without the power and ability to differentiate and to calculate the possible consequences). In each life the wrong behaviour led to a violent death. This is expressed today by inhibition and over-cautiousness when a situation arises where I feel I am being forced to do something and I am being treated like a child. The conflict emerges into consciousness later, but seldom manifests in the form of violence against things or against myself.

'RT was certainly able to explain the connections (down to the finest points which cannot of course all be described here). It is, however, only seldom eg in the case of grave traumas, that it is able to solve a problem entirely without something remaining to be worked on. Here, as with other special features of my character, RT uncovers the causes, but then begins the lengthy process of working on yourself, which neither RT nor the therapist is able to do for you.

'The scenes I have described seem relatively normal in relation to my present way of life and thinking, but therapy also brought to light the causes of the structure of several of my lives and of my present existence. These causes were discovered in two lives whose outward circumstances hardly make sense to the mind. First of all I saw myself as a slave. Together with many other people, I performed the lowest tasks in unimaginable squalor for a small élite, who had enslaved the whole planet. Brain manipulation and constant outside influence prevented any conscious resistance on the part of the slaves. They all wore a sort of helmet, through which orders were uninterruptedly sent out by means of a transmitter, like a space station (or a long-distance satellite) up in the sky which also performed the opposite function – by means of it, the thoughts of the slaves could be read. Certainly, I was not completely influenced; I rebelled and the guards punished me for this by beating me with whips, which gave out electric shocks. Since I would not give in and tried to make others resist too, I was bound, while still fully conscious, to a machine (a kind of lorry) which drove all day long round our place of work, which was in the open air. The worst part of it was that the other slaves were allowed to rape me and this they did.

'This most deeply humiliating life, subject to absolute force, came to an end in slow suffocation, when the vehicle turned over and fell onto a heap of sand. My consciousness – now freed – acting on a very strong impulse, resolved: "That shall not happen to me ever again. No one shall force me like that again."

'Undoubtedly, many lives later, this resolution led to my life as a magician who exercised absolute power over a small state, first through intrigue and murder, then by the use of herbal drugs and also through mental influence. All the people and the products of their labour served just to satisfy my need for power, which I enjoyed to the full. Beside this, there were magical works, which equally were intended to strengthen and confirm my power. However, even magicians are not immortal. An experiment with electricity led to the collapse of the room where I was. Great pieces of masonry fell on the upper part of my body, killing me slowly by suffocation and nailing my body to the rubble.

'In my earlier life as a female slave, resistance was obviously laid down as a basic structure, but was unable to prevail. The magician lived life to the utmost, but he still had ultimately to recognise that his power could not last for ever. This principle applied particularly to the misuse of my abilities and my power and fate made up for this in my later lives, when I suffered limitation, restriction and loss. To this day, my life is still governed by these contrasts, which are intensified by my constant awareness of the possibilities which exist (a general remembrance of my former power and might). RT has, however, rid me of my chronic stomach trouble – a direct result of becoming conscious again of the particularly traumatic death I suffered as a magician, when the whole of my abdomen and my stomach were squashed. Furthermore, when that particular life was being dealt with during therapy, I felt phantom stomach pains, even before the beginning of the death scene. This is a phenomenon often observed in therapy. It was only after this that the connection became clear. The stomach trouble I suffered for years in my present life was a warning to me to avoid violence in any form – without RT I would probably never have realised this.

'The reader may think what he likes about my reincarnation experiences and the conclusions I have drawn from them – I realise that they can be contested, because it is for me alone that they are of decisive importance, and they cannot be proved empirically. For this reason – and this is my final point – it is only one's own therapy which can provide proof of the effectivenss of RT.'

Elizabeth C: 'How I came to reincarnation therapy. My difficulties began about 5 years ago, when I was pregnant with my first child, a daughter. Up to that time I had not directly decided to become pregnant.

'I had, indeed, always wanted to have children and reason told me that now was the time; but emotionally I still wanted to put it off, so I stopped taking the pill and let "fate" decide for me.

'I then became pregnant when I was on holiday at the seaside. My feelings were very mixed. On the one hand I wanted the child (having an abortion would never have entered my mind). On the other hand, I was afraid of pregnancy.

'I became nervous, giddy and always had the feeling that I was falling and that there was no longer any ground under my feet. After the birth, things became quite bad. I kept feeling frightened and, especially when I was bathing my daughter, I was terrified that I would drop her and she would be drowned. I was scarcely able to do anything without my husband and often sat at home the whole day long waiting for him to come back. When I was alone I was afraid all the time that something might happen to me and my daughter would be left crying helplessly. In housekeeping, too, I did only what was absolutely necessary. I felt completely exhausted and could no longer sleep properly at night. I could not manage to talk over my problems with my husband. At that time he would keep out of my way, because I never did anything but complain the whole time. I could not enjoy life with my daughter at all because of my fears; when she was in my arms I was afraid that I would drop her. On warm, sunny days I always felt particularly exhausted. I found the sun on my head unbearable, I had a feeling of no longer being able to breathe properly.

'Physically I was healthy. I took various medicines for the circulation, which did no good at all. I also visited two practitioners who practise healing with natural remedies, without any success. Finally a nerve specialist gave me sedatives for a year, which did make things a little easier for me, but somehow made me dependent on them, so that when the tablets were stopped things became even worse.

'As a result of my second pregnancy (I could no longer stand the pill – it gave me attacks of anxiety) I did manage to leave off the sedatives.

'In the following period I kept looking for new ways, because I felt that medicines alone could not help.

'I sought out books, read a lot about hypnosis (I also had a few sessions of therapy – childhood experiences) positive thinking and then came to literature about reincarnation. After four years of serious difficulties with little improvement, I read an advertisement about the possibility of reincarnation therapy and decided after some time to try it.

'After the first part of the therapy, there was noticeable improvement. In particular, in the period immediately after-wards, for the first time in four years I felt so much better. My difficulties were no longer so serious and they were no longer chronic, but were mostly limited to certain situations; for example, the giddy feeling became noticeable again when I was swimming with the children, when I was standing still, when I was crossing a bridge, when I spent a long time with largely unknown people, when I had to sit still, or in any sort of undertakings which I really ought to have enjoyed.

'Above all, I kept having a feeling that whenever things were going well I had a "damper". If ever I thought that things are going well for me today, the next moment they would go badly again. I would often have the feeling that there must be a curse on me. Sometimes, too, there came into my mind pictures of arms, which had been chopped off and this made me afraid. (Twice I had this dream.) Before the second part of the therapy, I was terribly afraid, when going for a walk, that my son might fall into the water and at the same time I could not help thinking of children's arms sticking up out of the water and calling for help.

'I would now like to describe the regressions which seemed to me most important in the second part of my therapy.

'Regression 1.

'I am living in a house with my husband and my mother-in-law. I am, however, mostly alone with my mother-in-law, since my husband is often at sea.

'My mother-in-law and I do not get on well together; she rules everything and is forever telling me what I ought to do. Also she is always wanting me to have a child.

'When I do become pregnant a little later, all I can think is that I do not want to have the child; if I did I would be completely tied to the house and to my mother-in-law. I cannot talk about it to my husband, because he always does what his mother says. A proper discussion never takes place between us.

'I go to an old woman I have heard about, who carries out abortions. Her son is some sort of pimp. Since I have no money to pay her, she demands that I should make myself available if anyone needs a girl. Since I don't want on any account to have the child, I agree.

'The old woman brings me a herbal drink and makes me lie down on a couch. There she takes something like a needle and pokes around with it in my vagina. At first I am somewhat intoxicated by the drink and do not feel much; then the stupor wears off and I feel pain. Things are not progressing properly, I have bad pains in my back and in my right leg. Since everything is too slow, she reaches with her whole arm into my vagina and presses around on my belly. She says I should not make such a fuss, the baby's head at birth would be much bigger than her hand. Then she goes on just the same. I bleed heavily and then I lie there on the couch, completely exhausted. However I cannot stay with her long. I am to come back when it has all healed up.

'So then I go home and go to bed exhausted. My mother-in-law notices that something is wrong and pulls away my bed cover. I see that she knows immediately what has happened. She is furious and just says: "God will punish you!"

'When I am alone again, my conscience pricks me a little on account of what she has said. I wonder whether I have done right and how it will turn out. I already have the feeling of having done something forbidden. I still go on living with her for a time.

'In order to "pay" for the abortion, I must make myself available twice a week to a distinguished, rather elderly gentleman. Actually I had imagined it would be worse. Since it is a question of a man from so-called refined society, I even feel a little flattered. I always have to go to a room which is specially hired for the purpose. Since my mother-in-law does not know anything about this secret rendez-vous, and always wonders about me going away, she begins to spy on me.

'One day when I am coming back from such a meeting, she reproaches me, screams at me and hits me. When I then tell her that I am not going to give up this life or this affair and that this man is far better than she is, she throws me out of the house, so that I almost fall down the stairs. She cries again after me: "God will punish you, you will never be happy again in your whole life. This will always follow you, and things will be so bad for you that one day you will regret not having appreciated how well off you were here with us."

'I then try to go to the distinguished gentleman, but there is no one there. Then I go to the old woman who carried out the abortion, but she does not want anything more to do with me, because she is afraid it will all be made public.

So I end up in the gutter as a prostitute. Sometime later I have my hand or my arm chopped off because I have been stealing. It was customary at that time for this to be carried out without any further ado whenever anyone was caught red-handed. After that, my right arm aches all the time and men do not want to have anything more to do with me in that state. When I have my arm chopped off I think that this is now the punishment for what I have just done, but I also think that the prophesied punishment will come only after my life. I think that that punishment is the reason I lost my daughter in my next life.

'I do not know whether it is through hunger or pain, but at any rate soon after that I meet my end alone in the gutter, without anyone there to help me.

'My last thoughts in my misery are that probably my greatest mistake was the abortion and that we could perhaps have had quite a nice family life after all with the child.

'Regression 2 (the following life).

'I am living contentedly and happily with my husband and daughter in a simple little house. One day we receive the news that my husband must go to the war. He leaves us behind on our own; I have an unpleasant feeling and am afraid that he will not come back again.

'Later soldiers arrive and start plundering everywhere. My husband somehow arranges for me and my daughter to be taken away by ship to begin a new life somewhere else. I am very unwilling to do so and, as I sail away, am unhappy about giving everything up. There are other women there, too, with their children.

'After a fairly long journey, I am standing with my daughter on deck by the railing, when we come under fire from aircraft or from other ships. The ship's mast is on fire and burning pieces are falling down. I am standing there with my daughter in my arms, not knowing whether to run away or what to do. I am terribly frightened. Then suddenly there is a sort of explosion; people run about screaming. I believe some of them climb into a lifeboat.

'The ship, complete with rails and the deck I am standing on, suddenly collapses and I fall with my daughter into the water. However, somehow or other I succeed in saving my daughter and myself on a kind of raft or plank from the wreckage which is floating around. After a time I do not see anyone else, no land is in sight either, just the sun burning down.

'We sit on this raft for quite a long time, with my daughter crying and complaining that she wants to go home. When repeated explanations are no good and she still goes on whining, at some point I just cannot listen to it any longer. My nerves are all to pieces and in despair I shake her and shout at her to be quiet. At the moment when I am shaking her, the raft tips up and we fall into the water. I clutch at my daughter and she succeeds first in clinging on to my hips, then she slips down to my legs. Since I cannot swim either, I become afraid and have a feeling that she is pulling me under. I begin to kick out in order to get back to the raft. By kicking out I lose my daughter and I have a feeling that I am pushing her away. I succeed in reaching the raft, but I can no longer reach my daughter. I think that we shall both be lost in any case if I leave the raft again. I can see her struggling and gasping for air; I try to paddle the raft to her, but I do not succeed. Then I see her arm again sticking up in the air seeking help and then there is nothing more. I cannot find her again.

'I am completely in despair, feel that I am close to a nervous breakdown and then I am completely empty. I no longer feel anything. I come to myself again when the sun is burning those parts of my body which are unprotected, my head, my arms, my legs and my chest. It feels as though everything were burnt up.

'Then I sight land and think at that moment that perhaps I could have managed to save my daughter after all if I had realised that land was so close.

'I do not know how I do it, but somehow I manage to reach the shore. However I have a feeling that I must not stay lying down, that I must find some shade, since the sun is burning and I am anyhow at the end of my tether.

'I have to climb up a bank and I manage this with the last of my strength. I am quite dizzy with the heat and I am terribly thirsty. I let myself sink down under a bush in the shade and must then have fallen asleep.

'I come to myself again and find out with the help of natives that I am now on an island; they take me to their tribe and give me food and drink. They are kind to me, but in spite of that I am glad when, after some time, they take me away from the island again. Here I cannot stop thinking about the disaster. I stand again on the cliff and look out over the sea where my daughter was drowned.

'The natives take me by boat to a place where I can continue my journey to meet my husband. He has in the meantime been informed about the disaster and is expecting me.

'On the one hand I am glad to see him, but on the other I am afraid that he may reproach me. We are both silent and do not speak about the disaster, but there is something missing. We simply cannot be happy any more. We cannot have any more children either and somehow I think that this is my punishment for letting my daughter drown.

'I avoid speaking about the death of our daughter. We become indifferent to our life and our relationship becomes flatter and flatter. I have a feeling that, with the death of our daughter, life has ended for me too. We go on living but it is not a proper life. If I had been able to talk to my husband about it, I would probably have got over it better or worked it out.

'Regression 3 (my following life).

'I am living very happily with my husband and my children (I think there are five of them). I have everything I want, a kind husband with a strong character, who corresponds to my ideal, and very nice, dear children, with whom I have a lot of fun. We live in a wooden house in a rather deserted place. We are largely self-supporting, I look after the children and the garden; my husband looks after the cattle and horses.

'Sometimes we go to a cattle auction in the town, where I then meet my friend for a gossip over a cup of coffee, which is always very amusing and a welcome change. I am very contented with my life and cannot really imagine anything better. Yet one day this happy life ends for me in an accident.

'After working in the garden I go to a place a little way off where you get a good view of the neighbourhood. I am standing on a piece of rock in front of a narrow gully or chasm – I often stand on this spot – and I am so full of love for everybody, I have an indescribable feeling of happiness. At this moment I think it is this view which somehow reminds me of the place in my last life where I also looked out over the sea, where my daughter had been drowned.

'I suddenly have a feeling that the piece of rock is coming loose, I slip down and am just able to cling on to the rock. I hang there with no ground under my feet and cannot find anything to hold on to. Then the rock comes loose, I fall down a long way with the great stone after me and my skull is crushed. Death itself is not so bad, but I cannot help thinking of the children I am leaving behind and wondering what will become of them. Finally I also have the feeling that this life has simply been too good to ever go on so.

'Similarities with my present life:

'In all three lives which, as far as I know, followed each other in the order I have described, the life began well and ended badly. The explanation is in my opinion to be sought in the first life, where I made a great mistake in having the abortion and my mother-in-law's words followed me into my next life and the present one.

'Recently I had often felt that things ought not to go well for me, that it is really "better" for me to complain or that if things went well for me it would be all the worse afterwards. Actually the whole of my life so far had followed this pattern.

'My early childhood was really very happy up to the time when, at the age of eight, I lost my one-year-old sister. At that time I was looking after her almost all day long and felt like her mother. I am also convinced that she had been the daughter who was drowned in the sea in my previous life. I also have a feeling that it was her task to remind me about that.

'After my sister's death, my life, too, was not happy any more. Her death affected me very much and somehow I felt that I was to blame, although there was no real reason for this feeling. I was never able to speak to anyone about it either. Life went on miserably for me, just as it had previously after the death of my daughter.

'When I later married and worked, all went well again for me up to the time of my pregnancy, which I did not really want. I was not able to talk about my feelings to my husband at that time either.

'After the delivery, matters became really bad, because the birth of my daughter reminded me very strongly of my earlier abortion.

'The birth was artifically induced. I was in great pain and

was given an injection which was not any real use, or rather I felt all the pain in my right leg. During the whole delivery, a probe was fixed to the baby's head; it looked and felt like a needle.

'Finally the forceps were used, just for a short time. The doctor's probing was very painful; I had the feeling that his whole arm was in my vagina. That night also I was suddenly seized with a terrible fear that I might kill my child.

'With regard to my present situation, I see life number 1 as the most important one. After this regression I had the feeling that this was the "main cause" of all my difficulties. At that time I did not want to have the baby and today, on account of my fears, I cannot enjoy my children. My mother-in-law's "curse" reinforced it all. For me this also explains why things always got better for me just for a short time and were then worse than ever. That is probably why all the other treatments which I tried, failed or brought only a slight, temporary improvement.

'As well as this basic pattern, which appears in every life, parallels may be found in each individual life with my present physical symptoms and fears:

'The fear that my child might be drowned or my feeling of giddiness when crossing a bridge, when I have a feeling that I am just going to fall into the water.

'My dreams of arms and children's hands, which frightened me, can probably also be traced back to that shipwreck.

'The situation with my daughter before the raft tipped over sometimes occurs today with my daughter. When she kept on whining without really knowing what she wanted or when this crying would not stop even when I explained things to her, I could no longer bear to hear it and shook her. This frightened me. I knew all the time that my reaction would not have any result, but I could not help it.

'I constantly suffered from an allergy to sunshine, especially when I was staying at the seaside or when I spent any length of time in the hot sun. Indeed, in the last few years I always avoided the sun and always looked for shade. I would get little blisters on my legs, arms and the upper part of my chest, in exactly the places which were uncovered and completely exposed to the hot sun during the time I was on the raft. As for the feeling of no longer having any ground under my feet, I see here a parallel with life number 3 when the piece of rock broke loose and I could find nothing to hold on to.

'The situation in life number 2 after the death of our daughter also reminds me of my life since my "illness". I was living and yet not properly living.

'In addition to these similarities, which seem to me important, there are many little details (including positive points) which are connected with previous lives. I will not, however, go into these, since it would take too long.

'The "prophesied punishment" in life number 1 was that I ended up in the gutter and had my arm chopped off; in life number 2 that I lost my daughter and in life number 3, my accident, as a result of which I had to leave my children on their own and in my present life the "illness" which meant that I could not enjoy my children.

'As far as symptoms are concerned, the two other regressions in the second part of the therapy were of great significance for me. However in my explanations I would like to limit myself to just one life, since here the parallels with my physical symptoms appear very important.

'Regression 4.

'I am living with my mother in modest circumstances. From her I had learnt the use of herbs for healing and had thereby helped many sick people.

'One day some men come and arrest me for witchcraft. We have already heard of other arrests and also watched young women being burnt.

'First of all they take me to a cell, but soon afterwards there is a trial. A judge, a priest and a sort of executioner are present. I have to kneel on the ground and at every "wrong answer" I get a stroke of the whip on my back. I am supposed to confess that I have cast a spell on others, that I possess some sort of supernatural powers, which I have misused; but I am firmly determined not to confess to anything I have not done. I am already quite giddy and my knees hurt. Always when my strength is at an end and I am near to collapse, they pour water over my head. The whole thing is continually repeated, always the same questions and reproaches. After a considerable time the trial is suspended and they drag me out. I can scarcely stand and fall on my knees, which are very painful.

'Then I am taken to a torture chamber, where I am tied by my hands and feet to two bars. Above and below me there are sharp blades, wheels which are turned by this executioner. If I move or if I let myself fall or hang down, I could be cut. I, therefore, keep very rigid and in spite of my great exhaustion, try desperately to keep awake. I scarcely dare to breathe. Once I think I cannot hold out any longer, whereupon I feel the sharp wheels on my back.

'Just before I almost lose consciousness – I become dizzy and have the feeling that everything is over – this "executioner" stops the wheels and says that he is granting me a short rest. He pours water on my head again and then rapes me. He grins scornfully while he is doing so and bites me in the breast. I am in pain and have the feeling that he is almost tearing me apart. I loathe him and yearn that he might leave me alone, but it would have done no good to say anything. I had never been with men before and I am bleeding heavily. He says: "The whore has never had a man before".

'After that I come back to the trial. Since, in spite of everything, I am still determined not to admit to anything untrue, they say that they will do the same to my mother if I do not admit that I am a witch and have done forbidden things. Thereupon I confess it. Now I have to renounce the church with an oath. I know that this means that I am now condemned to death, but when they take me back to the cell I am at first relieved and am able to sleep well all night long. The next morning two men take me to the place where I am to be burnt. I have to go through the crowd, which has gathered, and then walk a little way over an empty square.

'Then I have to climb up some steps to a small platform, where I am firmly tied to a post by a rope over my chest. The wood is piled up below me and at the word of command a fire is lighted. I am terribly frightened, I am all alone, nobody helps me, not even those whom I once helped. I want to get away, but I cannot. I stand there, avoiding looking down at the fire, which is coming higher all the time. I become giddy when I see the burning wood under my feet: I try desperately to look straight ahead.

'Then I feel the fire first on my fetters; it is burning and painful and soon afterwards I feel this burning on my arms too and across my chest. I can still see the people there below me, but it all becomes confused and goes round and round. I feel as though I no longer have any legs. Finally I can only feel my head becoming hot and heavy and I have a feeling that all the blood is shooting into my head. Then I cannot breathe any more, there is no more air there to breathe.

'I still have the feeling that I must scream out loud, but I cannot. Then nothing hurts any longer, my body is totally charred and burnt until there is nothing left of it.

'My last thoughts in this life are that perhaps I should not have been so defenceless if I had had a husband to protect me. I also think that I have been far too kind and this has not done me any good.

'Parallels with my present life.

'What I find most striking here are the similarities with my physical symptoms, but also the fears, of which I would like here to name only the most important ones. I get pains in my back whenever I do something bending down, in exactly the same place that I felt the whip.

'On the days when I felt particularly ill and exhausted, I became quite giddy when kneeling or bending or whenever I looked down, so I would then always try to look straight ahead.

'My profession often required me to speak out in court and this at first caused me enormous anxiety, which I managed in time to overcome.

'The torture scene also reminds me of many things. I always used to have completely tense muscles all over my body and sometimes also pain in my wrists.

'More recently in particular I kept having pains in my breast, as if someone had bitten me. These pains also reminded me sometimes of a rope tied firmly across my chest. When I became giddy, too, I often had the feeling that I could not breathe freely, that when I was breathing in, my stomach did not come out properly, although I tried to make it do so.

'It was strange, too, that whenever I had had a really good night's sleep, the next day was so much worse (the night before I was burnt I had slept particularly well, the next day was all the worse).

'Further similarities with present symptoms can be seen shortly before and during the actual burning. First, I always had a feeling of fear whenever I had to walk over an empty square; but it was even worse when I had to stand still. I did not know then whether I should run away or what I should do. I also had a feeling that I must scream out loud, especially when other people were near and I felt I was being observed.

'My allergy to sunshine again reminds me of the places which hurt most when I was being burnt.

'Shortly before death came in that situation I could feel nothing but my head and I could not get any air. I have this feeling particularly often today, when I am giddy and become afraid. I then have the feeling that I am all head and no longer have any legs. I have difficulties too in breathing properly and I feel quite hot – my head becomes red.

'Changes I have noticed since the therapy began:

'For me the most important change was that I lost some of my momentary symptoms and fears. As I mentioned before, directly after the first part of the therapy I noticed a distinct improvement. If ever these fears do arise I now think about where they come from and make myself conscious of them again. This gives me the feeling that this is being processed and that in time these fears will be resolved.

'In relations with my family I no longer become impatient so quickly. I do not lose my temper so often and in general I get on better with my children. Also I have a feeling that they do not squabble so often. My son, who up to the beginning of therapy, would wake up every night, often slept right through after the first part of the therapy. Now he has been sleeping every night, which must have something to do with it and is a gratifying by-product.

'In the meantime, I can sometimes really enjoy life with the children. I am also much better able to discuss negative things with my husband.

'Not only have my actual fears almost disappeared, but I have also become much more self-confident about many things, which formerly were some kind of a hindrance to me. I am glad that I found this way and would always like to continue with it. I believe, too, that in course of time, through becoming more fully conscious, my behaviour will become increasingly positive.'

Fred H.:

'I was 38 years old when I noticed that I was not getting on as well in my career as should have been expected, given my education and the way I had applied myself to my work. The job I had at that moment, as departmental head of a large engineering concern was very varied and interesting, but I had been there too long, more than five years. In some way I had up to then avoided taking production line responsibility. Now that I recognised how necessary such a step was for advancement in my profession, no possibilities opened up, no one made demands on me and where I myself took the initiative, others were given preference over me. I racked my brains over the reason for this. Certainly I had problems with my fellow workers, I did not stand up enough for them and on the other hand, I demanded too much from them. However, I saw that the greatest problem lay in my fear of having direct and violent discussions with my employers. In some cases when I was attacked, when my employers reproached me with something, I behaved as though I were petrified, paralysed, even when I was in the right. I could not account for this phenomenon. Was it possible that during all my hard years of training at primary school, apprenticeship, five years at night school to pass the intermediate and final level examinations, university, practice abroad, PhD etc. I had failed to toughen my character, to develop my humanity? The strange thing was that I also became numb when my wife reproached me.

'A year later I changed my job to one with prospects of a position as a department head. After several months a very strained atmosphere developed between my new superior and myself. Viewed objectively, he was a typical "go-getter" with the hide of a rhinoceros. I suffered agonies, particularly since I did not defend myself properly but put up with the lot. It became clear to me that a change in the whole situation could not be achieved unless I changed myself.

'Through fortunate circumstances, I came to reincarnation therapy. In just the third session, after experiencing my birth and an incident when I was a monk in about the XVIIth century, which went very far to explaining relations with my mother and my dead twin brother, the following experience came up, which is characteristic of my symptoms of repression and my problem with authority.

'The beginning of the therapy is slow. I can only see indistinctly and keep looking for my employer as prototype of the oppressor. I think I am on a ship, a slave galley, I am sitting at a large oar and my superior is swinging his whip. Here imagination and fancy are mixed up. The event cannot be followed any further. I have a feeling that I am a prisoner, my feet bound together by chains, somewhere in a desert or in North Africa. We keep going round in a circle, baling out water. I am in despair, my home is too far away, I have a feeling that I shall never see it again. Life is treading me into the sand.

'Frau Vallières keeps going through all the events with me over and over again. She is not satisfied with unclear statements or impressions.

'She will not accept the reports until we have gone through them many times; their inner logic is correct and they no longer keep mounting up or contradicting each other. It takes a long time for a clear event to be distilled from them. As Frau

Vallières explained to me at the end, judging by the strength of the strokes registered on the biofeedback apparatus, this event is quite an important one, strongly charged with emotion.

'I am the leader of a group of legionaires. One of my men is a continual nuisance to me. My personality is weak, I feel that I am small and insignificant, cruel and tormenting. My fury against this one subordinate keeps growing. After a more serious quarrel, I stab him with my short sword.

'I am taken to court to answer for my crime. I put the blame on the man I have stabbed, on his behaviour. I am most reluctant to admit to my crime, I am all clenched up inside. "Yes, I know you are right with your charge", I cry inwardly, but outwardly I put the blame on the murdered man, on his challenge, his continual provocation.

'In the analysis which follows, to which Frau Vallières always attaches great importance, my inward attitude becomes clear to me. Life was cheap at that time. I believe that I myself have the right to determine over life and death, I look on types like that, who have annoyed me, as enemies who must be humiliated. I want to be strong and superior, I feel sadism in me, I would like to see someone die. The event has a very strong reference to the present. I suddenly realise quite clearly why I am inwardly numbed when I am attacked. The guilty event has been reactivated in my subconscious, no matter whether the reproaches come from my bosses or from my wife.

'I also have a feeling that the person I stabbed is my brother, Bernd. It occurs to me how often in our childhood I have stood before him so full of rage, hatred and scorn, that I would have liked best to punch him full in the face with my fist, but I was never able to do so.

'It occurs to me with a shock that the last time I stood like that in front of him was when we were about 20 years old; that when I did not hit him he let himself down into a chair and with his right foot kicked me in the groin. "Anyhow you are going to die of cancer in 10 years" he shouted. This occurrence, these words remained with me for days. It was as though I were fighting them off. Then gradually I forgot them. I have only just remembered that about 12 years ago, almost overnight, Bernd suddenly got serious pains in the testicles, became ill with cancer of the testicles, but did not recognise it and went relatively late to the doctor. He had an operation the very next day. It was our thirtieth birthday! A year later he died.

'Some further events, which I experience during therapy,

bring about a complete alteration in my understanding of myself, my inward attitudes and my feelings. And hand in hand with these inward "insights", the world around me changes too, although belatedly. The most decisive changes come about in my profession. "By chance" I receive a call from a friend, who offers me a job as a manager. I accept and am now enjoying all the advantages of a responsible, independent and interesting post.'

In conclusion, to summarise this report we can say that the law of Karma lies at the back of our difficulties in life. Joy and sorrow are caused by our own former actions. Thus Karma may easily be explained in one short sentence: If our actions are good, everything will go well; if our actions are bad, then we will have to suffer.

Karma means action. We can distinguish, according to their mode, between physical, verbal and mental actions. According to their effect, actions are either virtuous, evil or neutral. With regard to time, we distinguish two types of actions; intentional actions, which take place while one is deciding to do something, and intended actions, which are the expression of this mental motivation in the physical and verbal realms.

For example, I am now writing on the basis of a quite definite motivation and in doing so I accumulate verbal action or Karma. Whether these actions are good or bad depends mainly on my motivation. If I write with a good motivation, which includes honesty, respect and love for others, then my actions are good. If I were to write with the motivation of pride or malicious criticism, based on others, I would accumulate bad Karma. Every moment we are accumulating Karma. If we communicate with good motivation, a friendly atmosphere will be produced as an inevitable result; at the same time, however, this action produces an impression of one's own awareness and thereby creates the prerequisite for happiness in the future. Bad motivation inevitably produces a hostile atmosphere and this would mean for me that the seeds of future unhappiness had been sown.

Everyone is his own master and everything depends on himself. That means that joy and sorrow grow from one's own virtuous or evil actions; in other words, that they do not come from outside, but from inside. This theory is of great use in conducting one's life, for once we realise that there is a connection between an action and its effect, we will always be on our guard and check ourselves, no matter whether or not we are being observed. Imagine, for example, that you see some money lying around, which does not belong to you and there is no one about. You could easily take it. However, if you believe in the teaching of Karma, you will withstand this temptation, since the entire responsibility for your future lies in yourself. In modern society, in spite of highly specialised police methods, a few people succeed repeatedly in carrying out terrorist acts of violence. Although the other side has all technology at its disposal to observe and later track down the perpetrators, the latter become more and more cunning at causing difficulties and spreading terror. The real control comes from within; it consists in insight into one's responsibility for one's own future and in unselfish striving for the wellbeing of others. From the practical point of view, self-control is the best control against criminality, for inner change can put an end to crime and bring peace to society. Self-examination is of the greatest importance and responsibility for oneself has a practical use in that it imposes on us self examination and self control with a view to our own interests and those of others.

In order not to have to suffer in a later life, and, what is more, in order to reduce our suffering already in this life, we can by means of RT do away with old Karma and we can see to it that we do not produce new Karma, once we have recognised the way things are connected.

Friedrich W.:

'As a non-medical practitioner I have for a long time been practising "rebirthing therapy". An acquaintance of mine wanted me to give her such a therapy, in which I would work through her birth and then investigate the time she was growing in her mother's womb. When the therapy was almost over, she sank into a trance-like condition and from what she then reported one could conclude that she had regressed to the beginning of a phase of reincarnation.

'Since, up to that time, I had not occupied myself in a practical way with reincarnation, I brought her back to reality as quickly as possible and as a precaution I broke off the therapy. During this regression it became clear to me that this woman and I had Karma in common, because when she was describing her life before this present life there was a film running inside me, which made it clear to me that this section of her life had to do with my former life also. Otherwise I would not have known in advance the description she was going to give of people and places.

'In the conviction that a therapist should not begin a new therapy with a patient without having tried out the same therapy on himself, I came to take reincarnation therapy myself.'

Regression

Session 1: Subject of problem: Feeling of being exploited. (Q = question, A = answer)

Q. What could you imagine to be the reason why you always feel exploited? What could you have done to other people in that direction in a previous life?

A. I see myself on a ship, on a sort of galley. I am the owner of the galley and the people there work for me and for my interests. They row the ship. When they cannot work any more because they are ill, I have them thrown overboard.

Q. What do you feel about that?

A. Nothing special. It is the custom.

Q. Why do you do that?

A. I have married a wife who comes from a higher rank of society. I come from a lower social level, but I would like to impress my wife on account of her family. I would like to count as her equal.

Q. Where is your wife?

A. She is in my villa.

Q. Where is this villa?

A. It is on a mountain, or on a spit of land jutting out into the sea, which is in the shape of a woman's bosom with the water washing round it in the middle, so that the sides of the mountain go down rather steeply into the sea. It is just round this promontory that my galley is turning.

Q. What sort of a galley is it?

A. It is not actually a galley in that sense, it is a sort of cargo ship and the men at the oars are not convicts. They are just working for their keep (food and drink). This line of ships sails round this promontory from one town to the other. There is no connection by road between these towns, since all the roads from the sea go inland. The journey by ship from one town to the other round the spit of land takes one day there and back.

Q. What does your house on the hill look like?

A. On the hill there is a temple and it is this temple which is my villa.

Q. What is your wife doing?

A. She is in the house, chatting and passing the time with other girls, her companions or friends.

Q. What do you notice about your wife?

A. She is my divorced wife in this life. From her whole looks and behaviour it is undoubtedly she.

Q. What else do you see?

A. I am standing on the hill in front of my villa looking down at the sea and at my ships sailing by.

Q. What else do you see?

A. I'm not always on the ship, sometimes I am and sometimes the ship sails without me. There are other ships on the sea, galleys and warships. They must be Roman or Greek warships. I see the ships all having to sail past my spit of land, because there is a sort of shallow inlet.

Q. What else do you see, or what sort of a shallow inlet is that?

A. Opposite my hill I can very vaguely see some land, but this land is not important. Probably it is uninhabited.

Q. Do you see anything else, or does anything else occur to you?

A. Not really. Nothing else occurs to me.

End of session.

'Hours later those pictures from the regression are so strongly on my mind that I recount the whole occurrence to my friends. In order to describe it better, I even make a sketch on a piece of paper of my hill, my temple or my villa, and a sketch of my ship.'

Session 2

Q. What keeps recurring in your life, which you have brought with you from a previous life?

A. It is, for example, remarkable that there are songs or tunes which almost make me cry sentimentally.

Q. What sort of songs are they?

A. For example, 'I had a comrade' (soldier's song from the war), 'The other side of the Valley', (soldier's song), 'We are soldiers of the Moor' (prisoners' song), 'A paratrooper stands guard on Crete'.

Q. What moves you most deeply? What could have happened in an earlier life?

A. I see myself as a soldier in the Second World War, standing with a friend or comrade in a little piece of woodland, but not a normal wood. There are little half-sized tree trunks, stunted and crooked. It might be an old olive grove. Our rifles are leaning against one of these crooked tree trunks. My friend, who also seems to be my superior, is smoking a cigarette and says: 'Let's go then'. He throws away his cigarette, takes up his rifle and we go to carry out a raid. Actually I had been ordered to carry out the raid alone. My friend or my superior had only accompanied me as far as the scene of the raid, but I was terribly afraid of it, so my friend took over the job and during it he fell. However this action had drawn the enemy's attention to me, so that in order to get out alive I had to finish the raid and this I did successfully.

Q. What sort of a raid was that?

A. We had landed on a mountain with a paratroop group. From this mountain you could see an army camp or a barracks where about 30 tanks had to be put out of action. I blew up these 30 tanks. Presumably it is since then that I have had the song 'I had a comrade' on my conscience. After this successful raid, this 'achievement' was put down to me and I was commended for showing courage and initiative. Since neither of these things was true, I tried in my cowardice to be posted home and was successful.

End of session.

Session 3

Q. Something else must have happened in a former life, where you took it out on other people, otherwise you would not always have the impression in this life that you were being exploited by your fellows.

A. I see very many people who work for me, hundreds or even thousands of them, grey or dusty people, who are working somewhere in a quarry or a mine.

Q. What do you do, what is your role?

A. I think I am a sort of provincial governor or mayor.

Q. Do you have material advantage from it? Are the people working for you?

A. Actually they are working on commission from someone else. I receive money from there but somehow according to the output of these people, and not only money but also recognition, for I use the people quite shamelessly. Those who cannot work any more are simply sent away.

Q. Where to?

A. I don't know, they are simply sent away. At any rate they no longer work with us.

Q. Do you see anything else? Does anything else occur to you?

A. No, I just keep seeing the picture in front of me again, this mass of dusty, grey people.

End of session.

'These pictures went on reproducing themselves inside me and now I saw myself standing before a lamp with these grey masses in front of me again and suddenly I knew quite clearly that it was here a question of prisoners in a concentration camp in the Third Reich.'

Session 4

'I told the therapist that I now knew for certain that in the last regression I had not been a provincial governor or a mayor, but that I was some sort of overseer or commandant in a concentration camp.

'The therapist then tried to go into this life again and the pictures came back to me of my life as a soldier in the Second World War, where I had been able to have myself transferred home. There, on account of my "courageous" performance I was attached to the concentration camp as overseer or adjutant. I had felt myself rather superior, probably up to this point I had only been just an ordinary guard or soldier. I observed my "colleagues" helping prisoners to escape. I can still see quite clearly the hole in the fence of the camp, in front of which two steel bars were concreted in crosswise by the tank barrier, so that this cross hid the hole in the fence. The soldiers, who let the prisoners get away, did this only because they were paid in gold, gold fillings from teeth, jewellry or cash. I reported this to the authorities, so these "colleagues" of mine were summarily shot. As a result of this "faithfulness to the fatherland" I was again promoted.

'Here I was given a superior officer who was an alcoholic. He was slovenly and unshaven, neglected his duty and even slept off his fit of drunkenness while he was on duty. As a result of my informing on him, this superior officer was condemned for his conduct and he, too, was shot. As a result of this, I was promoted again and then held the post of commandant. During the confusion of war I was made provisional head of the camp and later confirmed as head of the camp.'

Q. What else can you see? Can you find out the cause of your death?

A. Yes. I see myself in my office, the door opens, strange soldiers come in and arrest me and the same day, together with three or four other German officers, I am stood up against the wall and shot.

'Enquiries I made later revealed that this camp commandant really had existed and that as an S.S. paratrooper in Crete, coming via Tunisia or North Africa, he had been transferred to a concentration camp. Up to this point the significance of the song 'Soldiers of the Moor' had not been clear, since this song had originated in the concentration camp on Lüneburg Heath, but no quarrying or road works were carried out there. After further research into this person, I established that when the English marched in, various concentration camps on the moors were evacuated, so that it was quite possible that this prisoners' song was then sung in other concentration camps.

Session 5

'Several attempts to discover a previous life were unsuccessful in this session, so the therapist tried to lead me into the life of a woman and this was immediately successful.'

Q. What do you see? What are you as a woman?

A. I see myself as a woman in a wooden house in the mountains. This old woman is a kind of herbalist. I see a lot of bunches of dried herbs hanging on the beams of this house.

Q. What sort of a life do you have as a young woman?

A. I am the young wife of a forester, whose mother used to gather herbs and I took over the knowledge of healing herbs from her.

Q. What else do you see in this life?

A. There is a knock at the door. Forestry workers bring my husband home dead. He has been shot by a poacher.

Q. Did anything positive happen to you in this life?

A. Yes. I am lying on a bed of wood and straw and I have a baby. My husband is sitting beside me, holding my hand.

Q. How many children have you?

A. Two, a boy and a girl. It is a wonderful feeling when your husband is present at the birth of one of them.

Q. What else do you see? What happened next?

A. The children go to school in the town. Our son becomes a forester, our daughter marries some official. I am alone in this hut and spend my time looking for herbs and using them to heal the people who come to me with their troubles.

Q. Can you see yourself as a woman in any other previous life?

A. Yes. I am the wife of a count. It is my task to arrange festivals and social gatherings. I see the castle in which we live. It is up a mountain with steep towering crags rising sheer into the castle wall. The castle has a great number of little turrets. I go to and fro down to the people in the village, collecting the rent for the land in the form of natural produce. I can see the landscape quite clearly, with cornfields and sheaves of corn. In my present life I do not know of any such castle standing on a rock, where the castle wall continues in the form of a wall of rock.

Processing and further investigation of this life:

'Some years ago I wondered where to take my holidays. I was not attracted by any country and I was surprised that about 2 years before I ever had the regression I should spontaneously have undertaken a journey to Tunisia and Tuscany.

'It was not until after this reincarnation therapy that I was prompted to make a spontaneous journey to Greece. Naturally I was again conscious that my destination must have something to do with a former incarnation, since – as I mentioned before – the soldiers' song "In Crete a paratrooper stands on guard" released sentimental feelings in me, crying or sadness.

'So I flew with my woman companion to Athens and from there I travelled along various parts of the coast, eg Piraeus. Then I took the ferry from Athens to Chania (Crete) and from there went by coach along the coastal road to Heraklion. Strangely enough, I apparently had no connection with these popular regions and coastal strips, so that it became clear to me that this part had no significance in relation to a former incarnation.

'The next day I went from Metala to Kali Limenes in the south of Crete. Here also I felt no connection. Then another day I went from Heraklion along the coastal road to Agios-Nikolaios. Shortly after the airport of Heraklion, at a completely blind corner, I felt a psychic impulse. I told my companion about this. As I mentioned before, she had already been informed of my experiences in a former life. Thereupon, she said she had already discovered something, I should wait until we were round the corner. Shortly after this, I saw before me the mountain with the tongue of land jutting into the sea, which I remembered from my regression.

'Now my psychic impulse was explained. It was a feeling as if I was being attracted by this mountain. At the same time this experience confirmed for me the veracity of my reincarnation. I drove to the mountain to see if any memories recurred. Opposite this tongue of land I saw an island slightly blurred by mist, just as I described in my regression. Strangely enough, there were two sailing boats sailing at this moment through the shallow inlet which I described before.

'I took the map and my regression was further confirmed by the fact that the coastal road was not built until about 50 years ago; before that connection between Heraklion and Agios Nikolaios was possible only by sea, since – as already mentioned in my regression – all roads led inland. Furthermore, the mountains and hills were geographically arranged like the folds in a crumpled tablecloth, so that connection overland was possible only by a very difficult journey by donkey or mule, lasting several days.

'I further noticed on the map a capital "L" which, according to the key, was the sign of a place of historical interest. The shape of the mountain, the view to the land opposite and the route of the ship from Heraklion to Agios Nikolaios were 100 per cent identical with my regression.

'On the return journey to Heraklion, I noticed a tank in a little wood of pines and olives. This at once stirred up a memory of another previous life. I was immediately conscious that this was "my mountain", the landing place of a German paratroop unit and at the same time the point of departure of military actions in the Second World War. Even today I see there is a Greek military zone on this mountain which is strongly guarded and fenced off and was presumably a strategically important point for the German forces in the Second World War.

'When I observed the little pine wood more closely, I saw that they were in fact well camouflaged Greek barracks. I was again conscious of the situation in my second regression, when as a German soldier I was standing with my superior in a little pine wood, from where the one-man raid had taken place. Now it was clear to me why I had had to come to Crete and why the soldiers' songs "A paratrooper stands" and "I had a comrade" were so important for me. The reliving of past memories from that raid in the Second World War, which had succeeded in spite of my cowardice (session 2), my rehabilitation, promotion and my final posting back home via North Africa to my work as adjutant in a concentration camp, had gone full circle.

Processing and further research into my life as the wife of a count or a prince:

'On enquiring about castles and fortresses on rocky plateaux in comparatively flat regions, my interest concentrated on the castles of the Loire in France, so in my summer holiday I went off again with my friend to find "my castle". As I thought I should start as near as possible to the beginning of the Loire Valley, I drove to St Etienne, but could not find anywhere to spend the night, so I drove at random further into the Loire Valley and arrived in darkness sometime late in the evening at a fairly large town, Le Puis. Here we were able to find somewhere to stay for the night. The next morning we had a look at the town and its surroundings and then drove on. At the far side of the town, where the road ran for a little way alongside the mountain, you could see into a side valley near Le Puis. Here I had another strange feeling in the region of my chest and my heart, since I thought I knew this place.

'As we drove on we got a clear view of a hill with a castle on it, framed by a small village. It was the castle of Polignac and it corresponded exactly to my previous descriptions. When we visited the castle, my statements about all the localities proved to be true. The pictures and descriptions in the regression corresponded exactly to reality.'

The following regressions concern a married couple (age at beginning of therapy: he, 42; she, 39) who, at the beginning of their therapy, had been together for 18 years and had up to then remained childless. She had just had two miscarriages, one after the other – after having already had two unsuccessful pregnancies – and these experiences had been the incentive for them both to have reincarnation therapy. During therapy a new pregnancy announced itself, which this time led to a premature live birth. At the centre of the regressions was not only the question of children, but also the relationship between the partners. It is perhaps interesting to mention that they are both psychotherapists, that they work together in an independent practice and that partner and group therapy is the strong point in their work. First 'Jacques' reports how overcoming an apparently banal problem led to the remembrance of an occurrence which has had a far-reaching effect on his present life. Then 'Veronique' gives a short account of the main reasons why her pregnancies did not go full term.

Jacques

A problem which I was able to live with, but which kept troubling me, because it arose in such an uncontrollable and inexplicable manner, was my fear of being too late. It was relatively unimportant whether this occurred in my professional or my more private appointments. I could hardly allow a short time for anything; for example, for an hour's journey by car I had to set off at least another hour earlier than necessary. If I did not do that, I became very tense and uneasy, although I could not give any good reason for this feeling. Looking back, I cannot see anything I have experienced up to now which would account for my being so afraid of being late. There have been no punishments or other unpleasant consequences. On being told to go back to some event before my present life where being late was important – early childhood, the prenatal phase and my birth had already been gone through – I suddenly remembered the following situation:

I have ridden away from home, from a log hut in a lonely part of a forest in the direction of a more populated part, in order to fetch provisions and supplies. My wife is in the last month of her pregnancy and has begged me not to leave her alone just now. For some time now there has been unrest in the district, there are enemies or mobs roaming around and it is a very dangerous and uncertain time. However, our provisions are at an end and must be restocked. I have been on my way for about half an hour, I am becoming increasingly uneasy and feel that I must turn back; but for the moment I reject this impulse as foolish and put it aside, because, after all, the provisions must be taken care of. However, after another quarter of an hour, I simply cannot go any further. I am seized by a feeling of panic, I must turn back. I am afraid that something has just happened at home. I force my horse to go as fast as possible.

When I am about 300 metres from the house, I hear my wife's screams. It is terrible – suddenly they come to an end and I know that it is too late. When I experience this moment, I cannot help crying, My God, it is too late! I see a couple of riders making off. As though paralysed I go into the house through the door, which is still open. On the floor just behind the door my wife is lying stretched out with a gaping wound on the right side of her head. I bend over her, she is no longer alive, they have killed her. Her open eyes stare sightlessly at me. I am completely in despair, life seems to be quite pointless without her. I reproach myself frantically for having left her alone, for having come back too late, that it is my fault that she is no longer alive. My eyes light on the gun hanging on the wall.

As if in a trance, I stand up, take it down from the hook, go back to my wife, kneel down beside her and put the gun to my right temple. When asked about what I felt, I say 'I don't want to live any longer, there's no sense in it any more, I am worthless'. I press the trigger, feel a bursting, numbing pain in my head, my body falls on top of my wife's body, I feel it going rigid and twitching, and I have the feeling, 'Now it's over, it's too late'.

While I am leaving my body, I have to review my life: it occurs to me that I have loved my wife very much, but that the relationship has been full of problems. I could not put up with her obstinacy. I would have liked us to have left the hut in this dangerous place long ago, but I could not convince my wife. She clung too much to the hut, which we had built together. We had invested so much in it. Before I had ridden away, we had had a quarrel about it in which I reproached her and said: 'If we had taken my advice before, we should not be in such a difficult position now'. That was why I did not want to give in to her fears now, and without further discussion I had ridden away, full of annoyance. There was also the fact that I was not too sure about her feelings towards me. For some time she had had a relationship with another man and left me not knowing for certain whether she wanted to stay with me or to leave me.

This changed when she became pregnant. For me this meant double uncertainty – firstly whether the child was really mine or the other man's, secondly the doubt whether she had really decided in my favour or whether she just wanted to stay with me out of embarrassment in order to give the child security. It was obvious that I had avoided clarifying the matter with my wife.

So much for the actual incident. The whole development appears to be a logical consequence of my lack of courage to clear things up. It took this drastic catastrophe to bring this deficiency to light. This incident has many links with my/our present life. The traumatic background to my 'being too late' is now understandable. The concept of being too late was unconsciously connected with the loss of my partner, for which it and the catastrophe were both to blame, and with the suicide which followed. For this reason it was only with difficulty that I could bring myself to admit the situation, much less to realise it fully. As if to confirm the connection between being too late and tragedy, later examples of being too late which occurred subsequent to working through these events in therapy, did not present any problems at all.

My suicide, which was linked to the loss of my partner, is a sign of a symbiotic need for closeness. On the other hand the violent words spoken to my partner are not to be overlooked: 'Look where your obstinacy has got us. Now you've got me on your conscience, too'. My incapacity to define my own personal limits, to assert myself at the right time and to carry anything through to the end, remains unresolved in this self-destructive accusation directed at the other person. It seems to me as if my present relationship with Veronique follows as a completely logical consequence and is in many respects a programme of opposites: when we first got to know each other on the one hand it was indeed decided within a week that we wanted to stay together, on the other hand marriage – binding us definitely to one another – was at that time unimaginable for me. Hiding behind 'sensible reasons', for example 'establishing a firm basis in life as a prerequisite', there was an indefinite fear of really binding myself firmly. That led to the apparent compromise that we were engaged for four years before we were married. The beginning, in particular, was a time of frequent arguments. I had a partner who remained incredibly persistent and obstinate in unresolved conflicts and who was not content with half measures. This made great demands on me to develop my capacity to perceive aggression in myself and to express it.

Fear of too great a closeness was probably the real reason for a strange kind of 'tolerance', which we then 'exercised' for about 10 years of our marriage as far as relationships with other people were concerned. We thought ourselves particularly advanced, because we mutually allowed each other to have occasional affairs. This led to even greater confusion in our own relationship. It was only when we had therapy as a couple that our eyes were opened to the ideological background of our 'tolerance'. After a final escalation, where our relationship was highly at risk through other relationships, which had now become very serious, we really found the way to each other. That was about 10 years after we had been married.

Now, in retrospect, this development appears to me on the one hand as a training in autonomy, a necessity for movement towards independence from one's partner; but on the other hand also as a particularly intense clarification of the real basis of our being together. There was a striking lack of both these aspects in my past life, as I remembered it. After the basic decision in favour of each other, there followed a phase of most intense arguments. It took us a long time to find out what the trouble really was. In the foreground – especially since we had dared to stand on our own feet by starting a combined practice – was the question of us equally sharing the work and duties involved. However it became more and more obvious that it was really a question of 'responsibility'. For a long time it had almost automatically become Veronique's role to see to the day to day necessities and to make sure that things got done. This often led on my side to a feeling of being supervised and restricted and on Veronique's side to the feeling that everything depended on her. It was only when, as a consequence, she went on strike that we could make any progress in this direction. Now we take it in turns to be responsible, one month at a time, for the above-mentioned organisational necessities and this works very well, although for me it is an extremely tiresome process learning to be really responsible and not preferring to leave everything to my partner.

It is only the regression already described which makes me understand that it is basically necessary for me to take back the accusation I made against my partner (which culminated in my suicide) to the effect that she was guilty of the loss of a human life, since I really had not assumed full responsibility for myself. Suicide as the solution of a problem seems to me today on the one hand to be far removed from my conscious attitude towards life – which I judge as a fear of difficulties – but on the other hand there are situations in which a pattern of self-destruction is still present – especially in aggressive arguments with Veronique in accordance with the motto 'If anything happens to me now, it serves you right'. However, in the interest of brevity I will refrain from giving any examples here.

One final point, which has a most decisive significance for me, I would like to raise the subject of 'wanting children', which will be discussed further by Veronique. After we were married I could at first think only with very conflicting feelings about our having a child together. Somehow I was afraid that the child might be more important to Veronique than I was myself. On the other hand I sensed a certain obviousness about Veronique's desire to have children, which made me afraid to voice my hesitation and my reservations. Also we had – mostly on my account – waited long enough for the marriage. Since we had in the meantime established ourselves well in our profession, there were externally no really cogent reasons why we should not have a child. I, therefore, had a very ambivalent attitude towards the first pregnancy. A German measles infection 'sent by fate' at the beginning of the pregnancy, was for me a sufficiently valid reason not to agree to having the child, which was on the way, or to the whole problem connected with it. My failure to relate to the child is a remarkable parallel to the occurrence I had remembered: there my relationship to the unborn child was obviously not important enough to make me realise that a child in the last stage of pregnancy might still have a chance of life, even if the mother was dead. The fear that the child would be badly deformed, which was highly probable, led – by no means without moral scruples – to a termination of the pregnancy, with the agreement of the medical authorities. At that time I felt only dimly that this decision against a handicapped life basically represented an avoidance of serious life problems, in the same way that a suicide can. What helped me to decide the matter, too, was the feeling of relief at having once again escaped the threat of a child. Against the background of the problems identified in the regression as existing in the partnership at that time, several things now become comprehensible. The uncertainty 'whose child is it?', the uncertainty 'is my wife staying with me out of love for me, or only in order to gain security for herself and the child?' and finally the dramatic climax of events in the fatal catastrophe may well have left behind traces of anxiety and kept somewhat concealed the desire which did actually exist, for children of my own.

I was able to become conscious of this desire only much later, 14 years later to be precise, when, after relations between us had been thoroughly cleared up, we suffered blow after blow in my wife's three miscarriages. My repeated feeling that I ought to have a child, followed by the sorrow, which I now felt very intensely, was extremely distressing and brought the whole problem, which had been in abeyance, to the fore again. The final breakthrough which made me a father came as a result of reincarnation therapy.

Through this therapy it became possible for me to live with – and handle differently – some quite definite blocks which I was able to recognise in the regressions I have described. In particular I became painfully aware of my own guilt in relation to life. I relived one of my former lives in which I was a woman and had an abortion, which broke me morally and physically. I was even more ashamed to recognise that my present decision to end my wife's pregnancy on account of her German measles was the expression of an attitude of mind which I had formerly held: in a life far in the past I was a doctor, who saw it as his special duty to eliminate those who were 'unworthy of life'.

Physically or mentally handicapped people, including many newborn babies, as well as decrepit old people were included in my euthanasia programme, which was sanctioned by society. My guilt lay above all in hiding behind what society expected of me and not heeding the voice of my own conscience.

Veronique

I would like to take the subject of childlessness and the questions which, for us, were connected with it, in chronological order, because that is the best way of bringing out the interrogational character of our reincarnation therapy.

The course of my pregnancy shortly after our marriage, which Jacques has mentioned, and the termination of that pregnancy, which was undertaken as the result of a German measles infection, were a violent shock to me. An abortion – for whatever reason – could, to my mind, not be morally justified. Finally I gave in to the 'rational grounds' which Jacques brought to bear. Viewed with hindsight, this decision produced a softening of attitudes, which has had a marked effect on my life since then. My picture of the world, which up to that time had been so conformist, was violently shaken.

It also resulted in my developing an understanding of many divergent attitudes and ways of behaviour on the part of other people. The upheaval also drove me to question the sense of many things and to tackle social problems, which had formerly been unimportant or taboo to me. Thus, through that decision my life has become much richer and today I am able to say that I would not want to turn back the clocks. The drawback was that I very much doubted myself and that – because in spite of all arguments, I was still led by emotion – I felt very guilty about the abortion. My desire for children, which previously had been so spontaneous and natural, now became very doubtful. For ten years I did not become pregnant again, although we did not use any contraceptives. I often felt that not becoming pregnant was, so to speak, a punishment for the decision I had made in the past.

Our relationship was outwardly intact, indeed we got on very well with each other in comparison with other couples. Yet something central was missing. This became obvious to us only after an intensive course of marriage guidance, to which we were driven by the escalation of outside relationships already described by Jacques. At the height of our last and most decisive crisis I had massive bleeding, which I did not at first take seriously. It was not until a stage was reached where my life was acutely in danger that I was taken to hospital. There I had something like an 'out of body experience'. I experienced being 'on the other side', I saw myself in an incredibly beautiful place, I heard the music of the spheres and sensed former friends beside me, telling me that they were glad to have me with them. However the efforts made to bring me back to life were successful. The first thing I saw when I came to myself was Jacque's deeply worried expression as he bent over me. This assured me of the deep bond existing between us, which I had shortly before very much doubted. From this moment on, we really began to move towards each other. We decided to be fully intimate and unmasked as pseudo tolerance the practice we had adopted of allowing other relationships. At that stage we were unwilling to acknowledge that the bleeding was a miscarriage, but later we were able to admit this.

After another three years – the subject of children having meanwhile been considered closed – I completely unexpectedly became pregnant. This was for us a gift from the gods. We were looking forward very much to this child, but by the end of the third month it was all over. We were seized by deep sorrow. It seemed to us as if the deeper meaning of it lay in filling a gap in our experience left by the previous abortion. At that time, as Jacques has already described, we did not inwardly want anything to do with the child, which was on the way, much less look forward with joy to its arrival. We, therefore, did not feel any genuine sorrow at its loss. What we experienced intensely at that time was a vigorous argument about our moral attitudes, but not joy or sorrow. To make up for it, we now had an intense experience of living with both feelings.

Many things which at that time had not been solved between Jacques and me now surfaced again. Among other things, a dream revealed to me that for 14 years I had unconsciously been blaming Jacques for being a murderer. I felt the presence of a 13-year-old child which was not to be seen and I knew that it was our child, which was not alive because Jacques had killed it. I felt furiously angry with Jacques and awoke crying out loud. In the discussion which immediately followed, I was able to express my accusation clearly. Now we understood what had been keeping us apart all this time. At the same time, once this accusation had been voiced aloud, it could be put into perspective, since my feelings of guilt became clearer. I recognised that it was a failure on my part at that time to delegate so much of the decision making to Jacques. It had been decisively our combined failure, as we now recognised, to have preferred not to speak to each other about our differing attitudes, of which we were both completely aware, towards having a child. This had certainly contributed towards the situation, in that it did indeed result in a pregnancy, but the child had absolutely no chance right from the start – the present clarification contributed towards the easing of tension in our relationship.

However we were in for an unpleasant shock, for after six months almost the same course of events repeated itself. Again I was pregnant, this time more sceptical but still full of joy and hope, which increased when the first three months were past and then, shortly after that, another miscarriage and again there was nothing more to be seen of a child. I plunged into a massive crisis over my own self-worth, from which I did not properly emerge until we had our reincarnation therapy with Ingrid. (For me it was a second course of reincarnation therapy, I had already had a course of regressions elsewhere three years before, which – especially since Jacques was present at the regressions – had done a lot for me and for the two of us. However, at that time the subject of having children did not come up, which is the reason why I have made no further mention of this first phase of regression.)

In this present reincarnation therapy it was a relief for me to find that on the part of Jacques, too, there were unprocessed remains of former existences, which hindered him from becoming a father. But, above all, for me, personally, several connections became clear.

In the first phase of regression I had already remembered a life in the XVIIIth century, in which, while a child, I was adopted by gypsies and later as a girl I had fallen in love with a strolling player, a puppeteer, with whom I wandered through the countryside. When I became pregnant – which was my deliberate intention – we broke up. Thrown back on my own resources, I tried in my despair to commit suicide, but I was saved by a wine-grower, who took me home with him. Shortly after this I bore two girls, both handicapped. Through a tragic chain of events, both children died in different accidents. My relationship with the wine-grower – regarded with suspicion by the neighbours right from the start – and the deaths of the children were increasingly the subject of rumours about me. Finally I was arrested and locked away. In my present therapy, the last phase of that life was worked through thoroughly. Horrible tortures were used to force me to confess myself guilty of the deaths of my children and also of some others, which were arbitrarily imputed to me. Among other things I was compelled by the use of brute force to swallow all kinds of horrible creatures. The worst part of it for me was while I was swallowing and afterwards to feel the slippery creatures still alive and moving about inside me. I tried with all my might to get rid of them and vomit them up. When I finally had the illusion of being left in peace, my fate was really sealed – I was burnt alive. This event made it clear to me that through the separation from my partner, through my suicide attempt, through the birth of deformed children and through the children's death, which was not actually my fault, but for which I blamed my negligence, the subject of pregnancy is for me unwittingly an omen of catastrophe. Moreover, as a consequence of the methods of torture, I have acquired a defence which penetrates right through to the physical level: a defence against every movement of alien life in my body. This accords with the fact that all my pregnancies ended before a certain point was reached, before the baby's first movements could be felt. Recognising and feeling this connection brought me great relief. I could accept that, owing to my previous history, my body had developed such a strong defence against a life growing within it.

This seemed finally to close the subject of children for us: we had never actually 'worked at' having a child, but we wanted to have an open mind if one 'announced itself'. Now, for understandable and acceptable reasons, this openness no longer existed on my part. However cathartic regression to the scenes in the dungeon had been for me, I still could not imagine after the revulsion, which I had just felt, that my block would ever be removed.

However it turned out otherwise; a few months later we were back in the same position, and this after we had for the first time thought very positively about adopting a child. We were thinking about a certain child expected by some friends of ours who were talking about an abortion. This clear decision in favour of a child must have been the final decisive factor in my becoming pregnant again. My experience of pregnancy was very much beset by fears that it might go wrong again, but after all had been well in the first four months and the gynaecologist had encouraged us very much by saying that everything was in order, we became more and more hopeful. Alas, it was not granted to me this time either to carry the baby full term. A trifling accident of slipping off my chair at the beginning of the fifth month must have been the cause of a so-called breaking of the waters, which even the specialist did not recognise. At any rate a fortnight later labour pains quite unexpectedly set in, which could not be arrested. An infection of the amniotic fluid – diagnosed too late – put me in great danger of losing my life and the baby too, it was struggling with all its might to get out and was born in dramatic circumstances after five and a half months pregnancy. The doctor said our son's chance of survival was nil, he was starting life in an almost hopeless position. The extremely premature birth – before the beginning of viability, according to the official definition – the high grade infection which he also had, an equally high grade of asthma, because his lung was not yet developed, difficulties in getting artificial respiration going during the first hours after birth, all this gave rise to a fear that his brain had had an insufficiency of oxygen. He had to be in an incubator on oxygen for nearly three months and to suffer many more very serious complications; but, as if by a miracle, he surmounted all hurdles and after nearly four months, just before Christmas 1984, at just about what would have been the time for a normal birth, we were able to take him home. To our great joy he has developed splendidly in every respect and is a darling, lively little fellow, who is into everything.

The circumstances of his birth were a trauma, which I could work through only with the help of therapy. The question 'why' was unavoidable. In regressions devoted to this question, I remembered particularly two occurrences.

The first one which occurred to me was the experience of a full-term 'birth', during the course of which I died. It was at about the time when the birth was expected that I became increasingly ill and lost consciousness and my husband took me to hospital, where they immediately said it was too late. The baby had probably died in me a couple of days ago – I had vaguely felt but had tried to ignore it. Meanwhile, poisoning had set in, which made it doubtful whether I could be kept alive. The baby had to be removed, which at that time was done by artifically dilating the vagina. Since the baby could not help, it was an extremely difficult undertaking. Whenever I became conscious, I tried to expedite matters by pushing too hard. At about the same time I must, as a result of the effort, have burst a blood vessel in my head, while the dilation of the vagina tore it and made it bleed. This event must have led me to connect a full term pregnancy with personal danger, hence my effort not to go the full term. Unconsciously I felt that a premature birth was a way of avoiding the danger.

It was probably right for me to work through all these things, so that I came to the danger.

The question which still remained open after the regression was again the question 'why?' Why did I have to die, why had the baby died inside me? I remembered a yet more distant occurrence, whose guilty significance still worries me very much. At that time I was living in comfortable circumstances and in a relationship where I apparently lacked for nothing. I was not in any trouble, there is really nothing I could say to exonerate myself. My life was perhaps a little boring, because I had no anxieties and no real work to do. In this situation I had a baby. This was my fulfilment. He was a very beautiful and extremely affectionate child, who showed me very clearly how much he enjoyed my attention. This developed in me a feeling which became stronger and stronger: it did me good to feel that this little being was completely dependent on me. I became completely intoxicated with power. Again and again it drove me to make the child feel how dependent he was, for example by withholding the bottle from him, until he was really screaming, etc.

One day I was seized by the idea that I was lord over the life and death of this child. I had given him life, it also lay within my power to take his life away again, without him being able to do anything about it in his dependence and defencelessness. I bought some liquid which gave off a poisonous vapour. At a time when I could be sure of not being disturbed, I held the child at bathtime over the poisonous steam. Before he died, he gave me a look which cut me to the quick. He must at the last moment have gathered what was happening. His look was a simple accusation: 'What have I done to you? Why are you doing this to me?' When my conscience pricked me, I quickly tried resuscitation, but it was too late. The deed remained undiscovered, it was just registered as an inexplicable death; but I was never happy again in my life. I was seized by violent scruples, my life appeared to me senseless, indeed I had forfeited it myself. Finally – when I became pregnant again and was afraid that everything might repeat itself – I killed myself in the same way that I had killed the child.

I have many past memories which are unpleasant for me, but this is by far the least understandable one. Awareness of the absolute dependence of a helpless being and awareness of having abused his trust, shakes me to the core. A massive feeling of guilt makes it understandable to me that in a later life a child I was carrying preferred to die while it was still in me, and that I died at its 'birth'. The present premature birth, with the dramatic attendant circumstances, could almost have been a repetition, but I could feel within me an absolute desire to survive. That was apparently good for our child too, in that during the process of birth I had shared with him something of this will to live. A strange problem has been solved for me after the regression described above and working through it: I was very much afraid of bathing our son. For some months after our son was home with us, I left it to Jacques or to my mother to bath him. I had the compulsive idea that something might happen to him if I bathed him. This worried me quite a lot. Now I actually enjoy splashing about in the bath with him and sharing his joy at the water.

In order to convey understanding of the case of Jacques and Veronique at sufficient depth I should like to explain things a little further. In the beginning Jacques' situation was as follows: he had a feeling of being pushed into the background, of not being able to assert himself enough, he felt that he was not wanted. He felt that he did not have enough to offer. The fear was always present in him that he would be too late, and when he did come too late he felt like a spoilsport because he simply burst in on a situation. Already in childhood he saw himself as a traitor, because he told tales about his schoolmates.

During his prenatal phase, the following significant sentences came up: (His mother) 'I don't want to be pregnant at this time, when everything is so uncertain. There is a war on. My husband doesn't want any children. Will he ever come back? We have had so little life. I am not too certain about our relationship. Is he staying with me just out of a sense of duty? It took him a long time to make up his mind to marry me. I'm really good for nothing.' (His mother collapses) 'Oh God, I'm done for now.'

Here, parallels to Jacques' earlier life can already be recognised. His mother is not sure about her relationship with her husband. In exactly the same way Jacques, in his life in the hut, was not sure of his relationship with his wife. 'My husband doesn't want any children' his mother had felt. Jacques was not sure whether he wanted children. 'We have had so little from life'. The connection in these earlier lives, both in the hut and in the gypsy life with Veronique (Jacques was the puppeteer who felt cheated by her pregnancy) was that their life together ended too soon, they had not yet 'lived'. 'It took a long time for her to decide in my favour' Jacques had said. He, too, could not make up his mind for a long time about marriage and much later about having children. Then there was the feeling of inferiority 'I'm really good for nothing', which came from his conforming too much to the world around him and from his lack of self-worth. While he was still in his mother's womb, he promised her 'I won't make any trouble, I'll be quiet.' After we had worked through the prenatal phase, we found the following event in a previous life.

'I am locked in, a bare room, thick walls, it is cold, I am shivering, it is useless to cry out, I've got no chance, surely it can't be true, they have caught me, they are leaving me to die, I'm getting weaker and stiffer all the time, my knees are stiff, I wish it were all over.' I ask him, 'How have you come to be there?' 'They are dragging me through the streets, my hands are tied behind my back, there's a chain round my chest tied to the horse, I fall down, they are dragging me, stones are cutting my hips. I am a stupid idiot, I should not have taken such a risk. I'm furious with myself, why did I let myself get caught? I was to get some information, I was caught in a trap. I am the advance guard of a troop, we have to capture a town, I have to find out the weak points. I'm over-confident. I imagine it is going to be easy, I've often done that sort of thing before. "Child's play".

We have crept up to the town wall, I feel there's something not quite right. It is suspiciously quiet. I stifle my doubts, why should there be anything the matter. "Halt, surrender, you cannot escape!" A whole lot of enemies come streaming out of the bushes, I try to warn the others, enemy guards come after me and seize me and one of my comrades, the others are able to get away in time. I am ashamed, I can't believe it is true that such a thing has had to happen to me, I am lost, they are pushing me in front of them. "We've caught you, you dog!" They take me to an open square and chain me to a pillar, they hit me in the face and spit at me. I am cowardly, want them to stop and cry: "Leave me in peace, let me live, I'll tell you everything!" I feel contemptible. The leader says, "We'll let you go if you tell us who the others are." "I'll tell you everything I know, how many there are of them, how they are armed, what they mean to do."

The leader says: "You've made it up, do you expect us to believe you? Lock him up!" I feel powerless, now I've given them all away for nothing, absolutely nothing, I feel so wretched. I despise myself, if only I could die! They push me ahead with mocking laughter and scorn, they spit on me, "coward!", they push me down some steps into the dungeon, I feel ghastly, so this is the end, I've made a mess of everything. They'll catch the others, I'm sorry, forgive me! (He bursts into tears) I didn't want to, but I was so frightened, they'll believe it's my fault. They leave me to starve, it's a shame, I can't put anything right again, it mustn't happen to me again, I mustn't be so over-confident any more.'

And these are the parallels to his present life. Jacques is still troubled by the fact that he told on his friends at school. He never wanted to stand out, he always wanted to stay in the background, to hide. He always lived in fear of not being listened to by others, of saying something which they would hold against him. From a feeling of guilt, he no longer had the courage to stick up for himself. He simply had no confidence in himself, he just felt worthless. In his life in the hut he made the following decision: 'I must not let the relationship become too close, to spare me this pain and uncertainty. I must avoid going away in annoyance, the outcome is terrible for me. I can't live without a partner.' This decision meant a fixation on his partner, but at the same time it meant that he kept his distance, out of fear of the consequences. His suicide set the seal on his unsolved problem with his partner and the lack of clarity in talking things over. It necessitated a painfully direct confrontation with these problems in later lives.

Now we will return to Veronique.

Here we find a rather different situation at the start. She knows what she wants, has achieved a great deal, but often feels that she has been missed out. She does not receive the credit and the recognition for her work, which she feels she deserves. Her attitude towards children is ambivalent, she has a feeling of guilt, because she is childless, wonders why 'no child wants to come to us'. She asks herself what she has done wrong. As the regressions into her life with the gypsies and her life in the hut show, she had momentarily given her husband the feeling that other men were important to her, although basically she cared only for her husband or her best friend. These difficulties in understanding each other were expressed by both sides as uncertainty and mutual blame. The recognition from the last part of her life with the gypsies (torture by being locked up and forced to swallow snails) of the connection with the unconscious feeling of disgust, when she felt life growing and moving inside her, was a decisive element in solving this aversion.

After looking into the dominant part – the feeling of not being recognised, we found the following occurrence: 'I hear stones rolling down, something must have happened, but it is not really anything to do with me. A building is being erected, huge stones are being fitted together. Every now and then there is an accident, people go crashing down with the stones. I am like a priest, a ruler, it is important that the building is finished, it will be good for my reputation when the building is ready. The idea of the building came from the rulers before me, no one has managed to complete it, it is too difficult. A thousand people are working on the building, twenty die every day. The sound of rolling stones tells me that something has happened again. I lay down the laws, the worship of the gods is important, everything works according to a definite scheme. The people are very poor and live in simple huts, hewn into the rock. As a punishment they are put on the building work. I refer to the gods, who want the building finished, but in reality it is for my reputation.

The person in charge of building keeps coming with complaints, I put him off by saying that it is the wish of the gods that the building is completed. One day he comes and threatens me vehemently, saying the building must be stopped or he will kill me. He has a sword with him. I am defenceless, but do not want to give in. I try to stall him: "I must think it over"; I say, if he kills me, he will be killed too. He says he does not care how he dies, whether it is as a punishment or on the building site. He accuses me of being inhumane, I justify myself, saying "It is for the gods". He is beside himself and yells at me that it does not matter to him any longer what I command, he stabs at me with the sword and says: "Your pride was more important to you than the people". I feel a short pain, then I collapse. After my death, I think: It has not been worth it, I have not really got anywhere with harshness and a need for justice, later on I shall have to learn what it is like to be in a subordinate role.'

Parallels: Completing something was more important to me than relations between people. I am annoyed when I feel myself disregarded or things which are important to me do not go right. (Today she is not given the credit for what she has achieved, because formerly she demanded too much from other people and treated them unjustly.)

Today I often get my own way too much (in contrast to her husband, who gets his own way too little). I am not good at admitting that I am in the wrong. In the other life I had also realised that it was not possible to complete the building, but I did not want to lose face. I also said that things the people did were crimes, when they were not, just in order to get more workers. Today I also find it dificult to admit that something is not O.K. I could still lay down the law to suit myself.

As in all intensive (Karmic) relationships between partners, the two partners are guilty of doing or neglecting to do similar things.

Veronique had oppressed people with her power as a priest, Jacques as a doctor, by deciding who should live and who should die. Too much self-assertion and dominance leads to too little self-assertion or to a repetition of self-assertion or else to ambivalence between the two. Both partners had refused to take responsibility in previous lives – for their relationship with each other and for the resulting children. This manifested in this life by refusing to acknowledge their desire for children and in an ambivalent relationship between them. When each of them took responsibility for their past, then recriminations against one another and acts of defiance and mistrust on both parts could cease and an honest and true relationship could be built up, on the basis of which there can no longer be any insoluble situations.

This example gives us a clear picture of mutual entanglement. There can be no intensive relationship between partners without Karmic guilt – the present relationship is an opportunity to work through what has earlier been neglected or what went wrong and to convert it into openness, acceptance and tolerance. The positive side of the relationship – which was covered over by the unpleasant experiences, is revealed again by living together and working on themselves – and can fully unfold. Taking full responsibility for oneself and for the consequences of an action, without calculation and without expecting one's partner to be responsible for one's own situation, makes a free and open relationship possible.

11.

Analysing your own Problems

A problem is a non-acceptance of reality. It contains non-confrontation, a demand and a firm expectation, an obsession as well as a fear and an incapacity.

In RT all chronic problems are analysed in this way:

1. *What is your worst fear with this problem? What is the worst thing which could happen?*

Example: problem with partner, disagreement in discussion, lack of understanding or not being understood. The worst thing imagined could be: no one will listen to my opinion, I am not taken seriously, no one is interested in me, I have nothing to say.

The worst thing one can imagine is always what one has already experienced in a former life, otherwise the fear would not be present as a thought.

2. *What is your inability with this problem? What are you unable to do?*

In the above case-history, the inability could be: not being able to support one's own point of view convincingly; self-doubt; not being able to express oneself clearly; lack of a sympathetic understanding of one's partner's mode of expression; stubbornness; not being able to enter into things.

3. *Every problem contains an idée fixe, which does not correspond to reality.*

One has to understand that mutual understanding and harmony should always reign, there should not be any strife. He should guess what I am feeling, he should understand what my mood is and show consideration for it, when people love each other, no words are needed.

4. *Alongside an obsession, there is often a demand on another person or on life.*

Nothing should change, everything should go on as before, wanting to be courted, to count as something special, to be spared unpleasant experiences, everything should always go well for one and work out. I want peace, they should leave me in peace. I want to live as a like.

5. *Every problem contains an apparent advantage and a real advantage. The real advantage is that through the problem one notices that something is wrong and that one must work on oneself.*

Apparent advantages are, eg avoidances. With the problem of 'shyness', the person in question avoids aggression and thinks 'shyness is not as bad as aggression. If I am timid, no one can get at me, I shall be left in peace, no one will expect too much of me, I can hide, withdraw.' Behind every problem there is a calculation, if there were not, one would have been able to solve the problem directly, eg a young man says he would very much like to win at a game, but he always loses. In these cases both the will and the reality are of the person's own making. In such a case you discuss the advantages of losing (since obviously the person does not really want to win or he would do so) and the disadvantages of winning (since the person avoids doing so). You find calculations, such as 'If I win, everyone will expect me to win next time too and that is too much of a strain for me', 'Then I shall come under stress, I don't want to arouse any expectations'. 'If I lose, no one will expect anything of me.'

Another example:

A woman very much wants children, but does not have any. Here, too, both parts, the one which wants children and also the one which does not want them, and which is expressed through the body, belong to that person's realm of responsibility. In this case you establish communication with the part which does not want children, since that is the more hidden part. Things come to light, such as: 'I am quite glad that I do not have to bear any responsibility', 'I'm afraid that I might not be a good mother', 'Perhaps the child would not get on with me', 'Perhaps I might lose my partner on account of the child', 'I would have to give up too many pleasures'.

The problem is the reaction between force and counter-force. Mostly we see only one side of a problem and deny the other, which however, expresses itself in reality. If someone wants to be rich and does not become so, then, on the other side, he does not want it after all. However he puts forward only the one side, he likes to talk about this side and not about the other. Therefore anything which a person repeatedly gives as a reason is not the real reason. People do not talk about realities, or not often, they are just there. However if one has decided on false reasons and put them forward, this becomes a repeated process, one has to go on and on giving the same explanation in order to convince oneself about it. Therefore, in therapy, the therapist proceeds on the principle that when a client gives a reason or an explanation for a problem or for some behaviour and keeps on giving it, that is not the real reason. If he had known the real reason, the problem would have been solved long ago, so it must be a question of illusions and half-truths. It is only when one has found out the real reason for a problem that one can also find a genuine solution.

Note:

As self help, in the case of all the things which one would like to have but does not obtain, ask yourself: Which part of me does not want it and for what reason? Why do I not allow myself to have it, is my motive unethical? Would my character suffer, would I perhaps become arrogant? Would I then be confronted with problems, which I do not feel capable of solving? What are these problems?

Considering these points, making oneself aware of inner resistances and clarifying one's real motives, can shed light on so many problems.